To Western eyes, religion in Ind
tangle of myths, with many diff
worshipped in countless forms. This complexity stems from a love of story-telling, as much as anything else, but it is only the surface expression of Indian faith. Beneath this superficial level can be found a system of unifying beliefs that have guided the lives of ordinary Indian families for generations. These are explained in a clear and easily understood way by one of the profoundest philosophers of East or West.

Rex Ambler
1981

*Other Mandala Books*

ANCIENT BELIEFS AND MODERN SUPERSTITIONS by Martin Lings
THE ART OF MEDITATION by Joel Goldsmith
BORN IN TIBET by Chögyam Trungpa
BUDDHISM: ITS DOCTRINE AND ITS METHODS by A. David-Neel
THE BUDDHIST WAY OF ACTION by Christmas Humphreys
THE BUDDHIST WAY OF LIFE by Christmas Humphreys
THE CENTRAL PHILOSOPHY OF BUDDHISM by T. R. V. Murti
CHUANG TZU by Herbert L. Giles
THE CITY WITHIN THE HEART by R. C. Zaehner
COMPASSION YOGA by John Blofeld
CONCENTRATION by Mouni Sadhu
CONTEMPLATION IN A WORLD OF ACTION by Thomas Merton
CREATIVE MEDITATION AND MULTI-DIMENSIONAL CONSCIOUSNESS by Lama Anagarika Govinda
ESSENTIALS OF INDIAN PHILOSOPHY by M. Hiriyanna
EXPLORING BUDDHISM by Christmas Humphreys
GURDJIEFF by Kenneth Walker
HARA by Karlfried von Dürckheim
I CHING: THE BOOK OF CHANGE, a translation by John Blofeld
AN IDEALIST VIEW OF LIFE by Radhakrishnan
IDEALS AND REALITIES OF ISLAM by S. H. Nasr
INFINITE WAY by Joel Goldsmith
THE LETTERS OF JOEL S. GOLDSMITH
THE LIFE OF THE BUDDHA by H. Saddhatissa
LIVING SUFISM by S. H. Nasr
MAN AND NATURE by S. H. Nasr
MANTRAS by John Blofeld
MYSTICISM: CHRISTIAN AND BUDDHIST by D. T. Suzuki
PRANAYAMA: THE YOGA OF BREATHING by André van Lysebeth
RAJA YOGA by S. Yesudian and E. Haich
RAMANA MAHARSHI by T. M. P. Mahadevan
RŪMĪ: POET AND MYSTIC by R. A. Nicholson
SAMADHI by Mouni Sadhu
SELF-RELIANCE THROUGH YOGA by S. Yesudian
SUFISM by A. J. Arberry
TAO TÊ CHING translated by Ch'u Ta-Kao
TAOISM: THE QUEST FOR IMMORTALITY by John Blofeld
UNDERSTANDING ISLAM by Frithjof Schuon
THE WAY AND ITS POWER translated by Arthur Waley
THE WAY OF TRANSFORMATION by Karlfried von Dürckheim
A WESTERN APPROACH TO ZEN by Christmas Humphreys
ZEN BUDDHISM by Christmas Humphreys

# THE HINDU VIEW OF LIFE

*By the same author*

THE BRAHMA SUTRA
THE PRINCIPAL UPANISADS
INDIAN PHILOSOPHY
AN IDEALIST VIEW OF LIFE
THE BHAGAVADGITA

THE DHAMMAPADA
(Oxford University Press)

# The Hindu View of Life

RADHAKRISHNAN

Mandala Books
UNWIN PAPERBACKS
London Boston Sydney

First published in Great Britain by George Allen & Unwin 1927
Reprinted eleven times
First published in paperback 1960
Reprinted six times
First published in Unwin Paperbacks 1980



UNWIN ® PAPERBACKS
40 Museum Street, London WC1A 1LU

**British Library Cataloguing in Publication Data**

Radhakrishnan, *Sir* Sarvepalli
The Hindu view of life.
1. Religious life (Hinduism)
2. India – Religious life and customs
294.5′4′0954 BL1228 80-40541

ISBN 0-04-294115-6



Printed and bound in Great Britain by
Hazell Watson & Viney Ltd, Aylesbury, Bucks

TO MY WIFE

# NOTE

*The material for this book was originally delivered in the form of lectures, the Upton Lectures, in 1926, at Manchester College, Oxford.*

CONTENTS

CHAPTER I

# RELIGIOUS EXPERIENCE ITS NATURE AND CONTENT

AT the outset, one is confronted by the difficulty of defining what Hinduism is. To many it seems to be a name without any content. Is it a museum of beliefs, a medley of rites, or a mere map, a geographical expression? Its content, if it has any, has altered from age to age, from community to community. The ease with which Hinduism has steadily absorbed the customs and ideas of peoples with whom it has come into contact is as great as the difficulty we feel in finding a common feature binding together its different forms. But, if there is not a unity of spirit binding its different expressions and linking up the different periods of its history into one organic whole, it will not be possible to account for the achievements of Hinduism. The dictum that, if we leave aside the blind forces of nature, nothing moves in this world which is not Greek in its origin, has become a commonplace with us. But it is not altogether true. Half the world moves on independent foundations which Hinduism supplied. China and Japan, Tibet and Siam, Burma and Ceylon look to India as their spiritual home. The civilization itself has not been a short-lived one. Its historic records date back for over four thousand years, and even then it had reached a stage of civilization which has continued its unbroken, though at times slow and almost static course, until the present day. It has stood the stress and strain of more than four or five millenniums of spiritual thought and experience. Though peoples of different races and cultures have been pouring into India from the dawn of history, Hinduism has been able to maintain its supremacy, and even the proselytizing creeds backed by political power have not been able to coerce the large majority of Indians to their views. The Hindu culture possesses some vitality which seems to be denied to some other more forceful currents. It is no more necessary to dissect Hinduism than to open a tree to see whether the sap still runs.

The Hindu civilization is so called, since its original founders or earliest followers occupied the territory drained by the Sindhu (the Indus) river system corresponding to the North-West Frontier province and the Punjab. This is recorded in the *Ṛg Veda*, the oldest of the vedas, the Hindu scriptures which give their name to this period of Indian history. The people on the Indian side of the Sindhu were called Hindu by the Persian and the later western invaders. From the Punjab, the civilization flowed over into the valley of the Ganges where it met with numerous cults of primitive tribes. In its southward march the Aryan culture got into touch with the Dravidian and ultimately dominated it, though undergoing some modification from its influence. As the civilization extended over the whole of India, it suffered many changes, but it kept up its continuity with the old Vedic type developed on the banks of the Sindhu. The term 'Hindu' had originally a territorial and not a credal significance. It implied residence in a well-defined geographical area. Aboriginal tribes, savage and half-civilized people, the cultured Dravidians and the Vedic Aryans were all Hindus as they were the sons of the same mother. The Hindu thinkers reckoned with the striking fact that the men and women dwelling in India belonged to different communities, worshipped different gods, and practised different rites.[1]

As if this were not enough, outsiders have been pouring into the country from the beginning of its history, and some have made for themselves a home in India and thus increased the difficulty of the problem. How was Hindu society built up out of material so diverse, so little susceptible in many cases to assimilation, and scattered across a huge continent measuring nearly two thousand miles from north to south and eighteen

[1] *Kūrma Purāṇa.*

hundred miles from west to east? It cannot be denied that in a few centuries the spirit of cultural unity spread through a large part of the land, and racial stocks of varying levels of culture became steeped in a common atmosphere. The differences among the sects of the Hindus are more or less on the surface, and the Hindus as such remain a distinct cultural unit, with a common history, a common literature and a common civilization. Mr. Vincent Smith observes, 'India beyond all doubt possesses a deep underlying fundamental unity, far more profound than that produced either by geographical isolation or by political superiority. That unity transcends the innumerable diversities of blood, colour, language, dress, manners, and sect.'[1] In this task of welding together heterogeneous elements and enabling them to live in peace and order, Hinduism has had to adopt her own measures with little or no historic wisdom to guide and support her. The world is now full of racial, cultural and religious misunderstandings. We are groping in a timid and tentative way for some device which would save us from our suicidal conflicts. Perhaps the Hindu way of approach to the problem of religious conflicts may not be without its lessons for us.

The Hindu attitude to religion is interesting. While fixed intellectual beliefs mark off one religion from another, Hinduism sets itself no such limits. Intellect is subordinated to intuition, dogma to experience, outer expression to inward realization. Religion is not the acceptance of academic abstractions or the celebration of ceremonies, but a kind of life or experience. It is insight into the nature of reality (*darśana*), or experience of reality (*anubhava*). This experience is not an emotional thrill, or a subjective fancy, but is the response of the whole personality, the integrated self to the central reality. Religion is a specific attitude of the self, itself and no other, though it is mixed up generally with intellectual views, æsthetic forms, and moral valuations.

Religious experience is of a self-certifying character. It is *svatassiddha*. It carries its own credentials. But the religious seer

[1] *Oxford History of India* (1919,) p. x.

is compelled to justify his inmost convictions in a way that satisfies the thought of the age. If there is not this intellectual confirmation, the seer's attitude is one of trust. Religion rests on faith in this sense of the term. The mechanical faith which depends on authority and wishes to enjoy the consolations of religion without the labour of being religious is quite different from the religious faith which has its roots in experience. Wesley asks, 'What is faith?' and answers, 'Not an opinion nor any number of opinions put together, be they ever so true. It is the vision of the soul, that power by which spiritual things are apprehended, just as material things are apprehended by the physical senses.' Blind belief in dogma is not the faith which saves. It is an unfortunate legacy of the course which Christian theology has followed in Europe that faith has come to connote a mechanical adherence to authority. If we take faith in the proper sense of trust or spiritual conviction, religion is faith or intuition. We call it faith simply because spiritual perception, like other kinds of perception, is liable to error and requires the testing processes of logical thought. But, like all perception, religious intuition is that which thought has to start from and to which it has to return. In order to be able to say that religious experience reveals reality, in order to be able to transform religious certitude into logical certainty, we are obliged to give an intellectual account of the experience. Hindu thought has no mistrust of reason. There can be no final breach between the two powers of the human mind, reason and intuition. Beliefs that foster and promote the spiritual life of the soul must be in accordance with the nature and the laws of the world of reality with which it is their aim to bring us into harmony. The chief sacred scriptures of the Hindus, the Vedas, register the intuitions of the perfected souls.[1] They are not so much dogmatic dicta as transcripts from life. They record the spiritual experiences of souls strongly endowed with the sense for reality. They are held to be authoritative on the ground that they express the experiences of the experts in the field of religion. If the utterances of the Vedas were uninformed by

[1] *Taittirīya Āraṇyaka*, i. 2.

spiritual insight, they would have no claim to our belief. The truths revealed in the Vedas are capable of being re-experienced on compliance with ascertained conditions. We can discriminate between the genuine and the spurious in religious experience, not only by means of logic but also through life. By experimenting with different religious conceptions and relating them with the rest of our life, we can know the sound from the unsound.

The Vedas bring together the different ways in which the religious-minded of that age experienced reality and describe the general principles of religious knowledge and growth. As the experiences themselves are of a varied character, so their records are many-sided (*viśvatomukham*) or 'suggestive of many interpretations' (*anekārthatām*).[1]

It is essential to every religion that its heritage should be treated as sacred. A society which puts a halo of sanctity round its tradition gains an inestimable advantage of power and permanence. The Vedic tradition became surrounded with sanctity, and so helped to transmit culture and ensure the continuity of civilization. The sacred scriptures make the life of the spirit real even to those who are incapable of insight. Men, in the rough and tumble of life with their problems and perplexities, sins and sorrows, have no patience for balanced arguments or sustained meditation, but they want some formula or rule of life which they can accept as valid. Through it, they are inducted into a new way of life. A living tradition influences our inner faculties, humanizes our nature and lifts us to a higher level. By means of it, every generation is moulded in a particular cast which gives individuality and interest to every cultural type. Even those who wish to discern the truth for themselves require a guide in the early stages.

The Hindu attitude to the Vedas is one of trust tempered by criticism, trust because the beliefs and forms which helped our fathers are likely to be of use to us also; criticism because, however valuable the testimony of past ages may be, it cannot deprive the present age of its right to inquire and sift the

[1] *Nyāyasudhā*.

evidence. Precious as are the echoes of God's voice in the souls of men of long ago, our regard for them must be tempered by the recognition of the truth that God has never finished the revelation of His wisdom and love. Besides, our interpretation of religious experience must be in conformity with the findings of science. As knowledge grows, our theology develops. Only those parts of the tradition which are logically coherent are to be accepted as superior to the evidence of the senses and not the whole tradition.[1]

The Hindu philosophy of religion starts from and returns to an experimental basis. Only this basis is as wide as human nature itself. Other religious systems start with this or that particular experimental datum. Christian theology, for example, takes its stand on the immediate certitude of Jesus as one whose absolute authority over conscience is self-certifying and whose ability and willingness to save the soul it is impossible not to trust. Christian theology becomes relevant only for those who share or accept a particular kind of spiritual experience, and these are tempted to dismiss other experiences as illusory and other scriptures as imperfect. Hinduism was not betrayed into this situation on account of its adherence to fact. The Hindu thinker readily admits other points of view than his own and considers them to be just as worthy of attention. If the whole race of man, in every land, of every colour, and every stage of culture, is the offspring of God, then we must admit that, in the vast compass of his providence, all are being trained by his wisdom and supported by his love to reach within the limits of their powers a knowledge of the Supreme. When the Hindu found that different people aimed at and achieved God-realization in different ways, he generously recognized them all and justified their place in the course of history. He used the distinctive scriptures of the different groups for their uplift since they remain the source, almost the only source, for the development of their tastes and talents, for the enrichment of their thought and life, for the appeal to their emotions and the inspiration of their efforts. Hinduism is the

[1] *Bhāmatī*. I. 1. 1.

religion not only of the Vedas but of the Epics and the Purāṇas. By accepting the significance of the different intuitions of reality and the different scriptures of the peoples living in India, Hinduism has come to be a tapestry of the most variegated tissues and almost endless diversity of hues. The Purāṇas with their wild chronology and weird stories are mainly imaginative literature, but were treated as a part of the sacred tradition for the simple reason that some people took interest in them. The Tantras, which deal especially with yogic sādhanā, or discipline, and have influenced the lives of some communities from the time of the *Ṛg Veda*, are accepted as a part of the sacred literature, and many Hindu ceremonies show traces of the Tāntrik worship. Every tradition which helps man to lift his soul to God is held up as worthy of adherence. 'The Vedas, the Sāmkhya, the Yoga, the Pāśupata and the Vaiṣṇava creeds, each of them is encouraged in some place or other. Some think that this is better, or that is better owing to differences of taste, but all men reach unto you, the Supreme, even as all rivers, however zigzag their courses may be, reach the sea.'[1] Hinduism is therefore not a definite dogmatic creed, but a vast, complex, but subtly unified mass of spiritual thought and realization. Its tradition of the godward endeavour of the human spirit has been continuously enlarging through the ages.

The dialectic of religious advance through tradition, logic and life helps the conservation of Hinduism by providing scope for change. Religion and philosophy, life and thought, the practical and the theoretical, to use the language of Croce, form the eternal rhythm of the spirit. We rise from life to thought and return from thought to life in a progressive enrichment which is the attainment of ever higher levels of reality. Tradition is something which is for ever being worked out anew and recreated by the free activity of its followers. What is built for ever is for ever building. If a tradition does not grow, it only means that its followers have become spiritually dead. Throughout the history of Hinduism the leaders of thought and practice have been continually busy experimenting with new forms,

[1] *Mahimnastava*.

developing new ideals to suit new conditions. The first impulse of progress came when the Vedic Aryans came into contact with the native tribes. A similar impulse contributed to the protestant movements of Jainism and Buddhism when the Aryans moved out into the Gangetic valley. Contact with the highly civilized Dravidians led to the transformation of Vedism into a theistic religion. The reform movements of Rāmānanda, Caitanya, Kabīr, and Nānak show the stimulus of Islām. The Brahmo Samaj and the Arya Samaj are the outcome of the contact with Western influences, and yet Hinduism is not to be dismissed as a mere flow and strife of opinions, for it represents a steady growth of insight, since every form of Hinduism and every stage of its growth is related to the common background of the Vedānta. Though Hindu religious thought has traversed many revolutions and made great conquests, the essential ideas have continued the same for four or five millenniums. The germinal conceptions are contained in the Vedānta standard.

The three *prasthānas*, or divisions, of the Vedānta, the Upaniṣads, the *Brahma Sūtra* and the *Bhagavadgītā*, answer roughly to the three stages of faith, knowledge and discipline. The Upaniṣads embody the experiences of the sages. Logic and discipline are present in them, though they are not the chief characteristics of those texts. The *Brahma Sūtra* attempts to interpret in logical terms the chief conclusions of the Upaniṣads. The *Bhagavadgītā* is primarily a yoga śāstra giving us the chief means by which we can attain the truly religious life. They form together the absolute standard for the Hindu religion. It is said that other scriptures sink into silence when the Vedānta appears, even as foxes do not raise their voices in the forest when the lion appears. All sects of Hinduism attempt to interpret the Vedānta texts in accordance with their own religious views. The Vedānta is not a religion, but religion itself in its most universal and deepest significance. Thus the different sects of Hinduism are reconciled with a common standard and are sometimes regarded as the distorted expressions of the one true canon. As the Mahābhārata, one of the great epics, says, the Veda is one, its significance is one, though different Vedas are constructed on account of misunderstanding. The acceptance of this common authority by the different sects helps to purify them. Those parts of the new faith which are not in conformity with the Vedic Canon tend to be subordinated and gradually dropped out. While no creeds and no scruples were forced to disappear as out-worn or out of date, every one of them developed on account of the influence of the spirit of the Vedānta, which is by no means sectarian.

If religion is experience, the question arises, what is it that is experienced? No two religious systems seem to agree in their answers to this question. The Hindu philosopher became familiar very early in his career with the variety of the pictures of God which the mystics conjure up. We know today from our study of comparative religion that there are different accounts of the mystical vision. Some Christian mystics declare that they see in the highest mystical vision the blessed Trinity, Father, Son and Holy Ghost. Orthodox Muslim mystics deny this triune conception. From such variety the Hindu thinker did not rush to the conclusion that in religious experience we ascribe objective existence to subjective suggestions. The Upaniṣad says that 'God, the maker of All, the great spirit ever seated in the hearts of creatures, is fashioned by the heart, the understanding, and the will. They who know that become immortal.'[1] Religious experience is not the pure unvarnished presentment of the real in itself, but is the presentment of the real already influenced by the ideas and prepossessions of the perceiving mind. The mind of man does not function in fractions. It cannot be split up into a few sharply defined elements, as the intellect, the emotions and the will. The intellect of man is not so utterly naked and undefiled as to justify the view that it is one and the same in all men. The Pragmatists have done a notable service to the philosophy of religion in pointing out that different philosophies reflect different temperaments. The Divine reveals itself to men within the framework of their intimate prejudices. Each religious genius spells out the mystery

[1] Śvetāśvatara Upaniṣad, iv. 17.

of God according to his own endowment, personal, racial, and historical. The variety of the pictures of God is easily intelligible when we realize that religious experience is psychologically mediated.

It is sometimes urged that the descriptions of God conflict with one another. It only shows that our notions are not true. To say that our ideas of God are not true is not to deny the reality of God to which our ideas refer. Refined definitions of God as moral personality, and holy love may contradict cruder ones which look upon him as a primitive despot, a sort of sultan in the sky, but they all intend the same reality. If personal equation does not vitiate the claim to objectivity in sense perception and scientific inquiry, there is no reason to assume that it does so in religious experience.

The Hindu never doubted the reality of the one supreme universal spirit, however much the descriptions of it may fall short of its nature. Whatever the doctrinaires may say, the saints of God are anxious to affirm that much is hidden from their sight. God hideth himself. It is a sound religious agnosticism which bids us hold our peace regarding the nature of the supreme spirit. Silence is more significant than speech regarding the depths of the divine. The altars erected to the unknown gods in the Græco-Roman world were but an expression of man's ignorance of the divine nature. The sense of failure in man's quest for the unseen is symbolized by them. When asked to define the nature of God, the seer of the Upaniṣad sat silent, and when pressed to answer exclaimed that the Absolute is silence. The mystery of the divine reality eludes the machinery of speech and symbol. The 'Divine Darkness', 'That of which nothing can be said', and such other expressions are used by the devout when they attempt to describe their consciousness of direct communion with God.

The Hindu thinkers bring out the sense of the otherness of the divine by the use of negatives, 'There the eye goes not, speech goes not, nor mind, we know not, we understand not how one would teach it.'[1] The *neti*, 'not this', of Yājñavalkya

[1] *Kena Upaniṣad*, 3.

reminds us of the *nescio* of Bernard, of 'the dim silence where all lovers lose themselves' of Ruysbroeck, of the negative descriptions of Dionysius the Aeropagite, Eckhart and Boehme.

But the human mind finds it extremely difficult to resign itself to absolute silence or negative descriptions. Man is a talking animal. He insists on interpreting the religious mystery in terms of his own experience. The completely other, the absolutely unlimited, seems to be akin to the utterly indefinite. The human mind craves for something definite and limited and so uses its resources for bringing down the Supreme to the region of the determined. We cannot think of God without using our imagination. The religious seer needs the help of the imagination to express his vision. 'Without a parable spake he not unto them.' The highest category we can use is that of self-conscious personality. We are persons, *puruṣas*, and God is perfect personality (*uttama puruṣa*). If we analyse the concept of personality, we find that it includes cognition, emotion, and will, and God is viewed as the supreme knower, the great lover, and the perfect will, Brahmā, Viṣṇu, Śiva. These are not three independent centres of consciousness, as popular theology represents, but three sides of one complex personality. The different pictures of God which prevailed in the country were affiliated to one or the other of this trinity.

The soul of man is complex in character and so is the environment. The reactions of an infinite soul to an infinite environment cannot be limited to this or that formula. When we suffer from the pressure of the finite, we take refuge in the infinite. The finite presses on us at so many different points, and our different accounts of God are the outcome of this protean pressure. 'Such as men themselves are, such will God Himself seem to them to be', says the Cambridge Platonist, John Smith. The seers of the Upaniṣads were impressed by the unreality of the world, its fleeting and transitory character, and sought for the infinite real, the *sat* which would not roll away like the mists of *māyā*, or illusion. The sorrow and the suffering of the world cut into the soul of the Buddha and added a poignancy to his conviction of the unreality of finite things, and he found an escape from it in the eternal dharma, or righteousness. The inversion of the moral values affected the Hebrew most, and he found relief in an omnipotent and just God, who would destroy the wicked and save the righteous. The Hebrew prophets and Mahomet were struck by the majesty and the unconditional binding force of the imperative of conscience. Since they were familiar with kingship as the source of all authority, they made the supreme a lord of lords, a king of kings. The Protestant Christians do not care so much for the inviolable dignity of the ethical imperative as for the essential benignity and beneficence of the Supreme. God is our Father in heaven and we are his prodigal sons who have wandered from him, though he is ever ready to welcome us with rejoicing the moment we are willing to return. While fathers are just, mothers are merciful, and so the Catholic Christians and the Śāktas look upon God as the Mother, whose compassionate heart pours itself for the child out of vātsalya, or the love analogous to that of the cow for the calf, whose impurities she licks away. Every view of God from the primitive worship of nature up to the Father-love of a St Francis and the Mother-love of a Rāmakṛṣṇa represents some aspect or other of the relation of the human to the divine spirit. Each method of approach, each mode of address answers to some mood of the human mind. Not one of them gives the whole truth, though each of them is partially true. God is more than the law that commands, the judge that condemns, the love that constrains, the father to whom we owe our being, or the mother with whom is bound up all that we can hope for or aspire to. 'Him who is the One Real sages name variously.'[1] 'My names are many as declared by the great seers.'[2] To admit the various descriptions of God is not to lapse into polytheism. When Yājñavalkya was called upon to state the number of gods, he started with the popular number 3306, and ended by reducing them all to one Brahman. 'This indestructible enduring reality is to be looked upon as one only.'[3]

[1] *Ṛg Veda*, i. 164. 46.
[2] *Mahābhārata*. Sānti parva.
[3] *Bṛhadāraṇyaka Up.*, iv.4. 20.

These different representations do not tell us about what God is in himself but only what he is to us. The anthropomorphic conception of the divine is relative to our needs. We look upon God as interested in flowers and stars, little birds and children, in broken hearts and in binding them up. But God exists for himself and not merely for us. To look upon God as an instrument for the advancement of human ends is to exaggerate our own importance. We seem to give value to God, more than God to us. Tukārām says, 'That we fall into sin is thy good fortune: we have bestowed name and form on thee; had it not been we, who would have asked after thee, when thou wast lonely and unembodied? It is the darkness that makes the light shine, the setting that gives lustre to the gem. Disease brought to light Dhanvantari; why should a healthy man wish to know him? It is poison that confers its value on nectar; gold and brass are high or low compared with each other. Tuka says, know this, O God, that because we exist, Godhead has been conferred on you.'[1] What constitutes existence for others is not what constitutes existence for oneself.

Every attempt at solving the problem of the ultimate basis of existence from a religious point of view has come to admit an Absolute or God. Rationalistic logic and mystic contemplation favour as a rule the former conception, while ethical theism is disposed to the latter. It has been so in Hindu thought from the age of the Upaniṣads till the present day. We find the same ambiguity in Christianity. The personal category is transcended in the highest experiences of the Christian mystics. Hinduism affirms that some of the highest and richest manifestations which religion has produced require a personal God. There is a rational compulsion to postulate the personality of the divine. While Hindu thought does justice to the personal aspect of the Supreme, it does not allow us to forget the supra-personal character of the central reality. Even those who admit the personal conception of God urge that there are heights and depths in the being of God which are beyond our comprehension. The supreme cause and ground and end of the

[1] *Tukārām*, iii. 87.

world is certainly not less than what we know as self-conscious personality. Only it is not an object among objects, or a subject among subjects, but is the immanent ground and operative principle in all subjects and objects. The supra-personal and the personal representations of the real are the absolute and the relative ways of expressing the one reality. When we emphasize the nature of reality in itself we get the absolute Brahman; when we emphasize its relation to us we get the personal Bhagavān.[1]

Hindu thought believes in the evolution of our knowledge of of God. We have to vary continually our notions of God until we pass beyond all notions into the heart of the reality itself, which our ideas endeavour to report. Hinduism does not distinguish ideas of God as true and false, adopting one particular idea as the standard for the whole human race. It accepts the obvious fact that mankind seeks its goal of God at various levels and in various directions, and feels sympathy with every stage of the search. The same God expresses itself at one stage as power, at another as personality, at a third as all-comprehensive spirit, just as the same forces which put forth the green leaves also cause the crimson flowers to grow. We do not say that the crimson flowers are all the truth and the green leaves are all false. Hinduism accepts all religious notions as facts and arranges them in the order of their more or less intrinsic significance. The bewildering polytheism of the masses and the uncompromising montheism of the classes are for the Hindu the expressions of one and the same force at different levels. Hinduism insists on our working steadily upwards and improving our knowledge of God. 'The worshippers of the Absolute are the highest in rank; second to them are the worshippers of the personal God; then come the worshippers of the incarnations like Rāma, Kṛṣṇa, Buddha; below them are those who worship ancestors, deities and sages, and lowest of all are the worshippers of the petty forces and spirits.' Again, 'The deities of some men are in water (i.e. bathing-places), those of the more advanced are in the heavens, those of the children (in

[1] *Bhāgavata.*

religion) are in images of wood and stone, but the sage finds his God in his deeper self.' 'The man of action finds his God in fire, the man of feeling in the heart, and the feeble-minded in the idol, but the strong in spirit find God everywhere.' The seers see the Supreme in the self, and not in images.

It is, however, unfortunately the case that the majority of the Hindus do not insist on this graduated scale but acquiesce in admittedly unsatisfactory conceptions of God. The cultivated tolerate popular notions as inadequate signs and shadows of the incomprehensible, but the people at large believe them to be justified and authorized. It is true that the thinking Hindu desires to escape from the confusion of the gods into the silence of the Supreme, but the crowd still stands gazing at the heavens. In the name of toleration we have carefully protected superstitious rites and customs. Even those who have a clear perception of religious values indulge in practices which are inconsistent with their professions on the comfortable assumption that superiority should not breed want of sympathy for those who are not up to the mark. There has not been in recent times any serious and systematic endeavour to raise the mental level of the masses and place the whole Hindu population on a higher spiritual plane. It is necessary for the Hindu leaders to hold aloft the highest conception of God and work steadily on the minds of the worshippers so as to effect an improvement in their conceptions. The temples, shrines and sanctuaries with which the whole land is covered may be used not only as places of prayer and altars of worship, but as seats of learning and schools of thought which can undertake the spiritual direction of the Hindus.

CHAPTER II

# CONFLICT OF RELIGIONS THE HINDU ATTITUDE

STUDENTS of mysticism are impressed by the universality of the mystic experience, though the differences in the formulations of it are by no means unimportant. The mystics of the world, whether Hindu, Christian or Muslim, belong to the same brotherhood and have a striking family likeness. Miss Evelyn Underhill writes: 'Though mystical theologies of the East and the West differ widely—though the ideal of life which they hold out to the soul differ too—yet in the experience of the saint this conflict is seen to be transcended. When the love of God is reached, divergencies become impossible, for the soul has passed beyond the sphere of the manifold and is immersed in the one Reality.'[1] Judged by the characteristic religious experience, St John and St Paul have not any material advantage over Plotinus and Śaṁkara. 'One cannot honestly say,' observes Miss Underhill, 'that there is any wide difference between the Brahmin, the Sufi or the Christian mystics at their best.'[2] A hostile critic of mysticism, Hermann, the German theologian, endorses this view from his own standpoint. Regarding Christian mystics he remarks, 'Whenever the religious feeling in them soars to its highest flights, then they are torn loose from Christ and float away in precisely the same realm with the non-Christian mystics of all ages.'[3] Again, 'Augustine wrote a work of fifteen books on the Trinity, yet when he stood with his mother at the window of the house at Ostia and sought to express the profound sense he felt of being in the grasp of

[1] Introduction to the *Autobigraphy of Devendranath Tagore*, p. xl.
[2] *Essentials of Mysticism* (1920), p. 4.
[3] *The Communion of the Christian with God.*

God, he spoke not of the Trinity, but of the one God in whose presence the soul is lifted above itself and above all words and signs.'[1]

It matters not whether the seer who has the insight has dreamed his way to the truth in the shadow of the temple or the tabernacle, the church or the mosque. Those who have seen the radiant vision of the Divine protest against the exaggerated importance attached to outward forms. They speak a language which unites all worshippers as surely as the dogmas of the doctors divide. The true seer is gifted with a universality of outlook, and a certain sensitiveness to the impulses and emotions which dominate the rich and varied human nature. He whose consciousness is anchored in God cannot deny any expression of life as utterly erroneous. He is convinced of the inexhaustibility of the nature of God and the infinite number of its possible manifestations.

The intellectual representations of the religious mystery are relative and symbolic. As Plato would say, our accounts of God are likely stories, but all the same legendary. Not one of them is full and final. We are like little children on the seashore trying to fill our shells with water from the sea. While we cannot exhaust the waters of the deep by means of our shells, every drop that we attempt to gather into our tiny shells is a part of the authentic waters. Our intellectual representations differ simply because they bring out different facets of the one central reality. From the Ṛṣis, or seers, of the Upaniṣads down to Tagore and Gandhi, the Hindu has acknowledged that truth wears vestures of many colours and speaks in strange tongues. The mystics of other denominations have also testified to this. Boehme says: 'Consider the birds in our forests, they praise God each in his own way, in diverse tones and fashions. Think you God is vexed by this diversity and desires to silence discordant voices? All the forms of being are dear to the infinite Being Himself.' Look at this Sufi utterance in the translation of Professor Browne of Cambridge:

[1] Ibid., p. 29.

*Beaker or flagon, or bowl or jar,*
*Clumsy or slender, coarse or fine;*
*However the potter may make or mar,*
*All were made to contain the wine:*
*Should we seek this one or that one shun*
*When the wine which gives them their worth is one?*

Bearing in mind this great truth, Hinduism developed an attitude of comprehensive charity instead of a fanatic faith in an inflexible creed. It accepted the multiplicity of aboriginal gods and others which originated, most of them, outside the Aryan tradition, and justified them all. It brought together into one whole all believers in God. Many sects professing many different beliefs live within the Hindu fold. Heresy-hunting, the favourite game or many religions, is singularly absent from Hinduism.

Hinduism is wholly free from the strange obsession of some faiths that the acceptance of a particular religious metaphysic is necessary for salvation, and non-acceptance thereof is a heinous sin meriting eternal punishment in hell. Here and there outbursts of sectarian fanaticism are found recorded in the literature of the Hindus, which indicate the first effects of the conflicts of the different groups brought together into the one fold; but the main note of Hinduism is one of respect and good will for other creeds. When a worshipper of Viṣṇu had a feeling in his heart against a worshipper of Śiva and he bowed before the image of Viṣṇu, the face of the image divided itself in half and Śiva appeared on one side and Viṣṇu on the other, and the two smiling as one face on the bigoted worshipper told him that Viṣṇu and Śiva were one. The story is significant.

In a sense, Hinduism may be regarded as the first example in the world of a missionary religion. Only its missionary spirit is different from that associated with the proselytizing creeds. It did not regard it as its mission to convert humanity to any one opinion. For what counts is conduct and not belief. Worshippers of different gods and followers of different rites were taken into the Hindu fold. Kṛṣṇa, according to the

*Bhagavadgītā*, accepts as his own, not only the oppressed classes, women and Śūdras, but even those of unclean descent (*pāpayonayaḥ*), like the Kirātas and the Hūṇas. The ancient practice of Vrātyastoma, described fully in the *Tāṇḍya Brāhmaṇa*, shows that not only individuals but whole tribes were absorbed into Hinduism.[1]

When in the hour of their triumph the Aryans made up with their dangerous though vanquished rivals, they did not sneer at their relatively crude cults. The native inhabitants of North India clothed the naked forces of nature with the gorgeous drapery of a mythic fancy, and fashioned a train of gods and goddesses, of spirits and elves out of the shifting panorama of nature, and the Vedic Aryans accepted them all and set them side by side with the heavenly host to which they themselves looked with awe and admiration. It was enough for them that those crude objects were regarded by their adherents as sources of the supreme blessings of life and centres of power which can be drawn upon. The gods of the *Ṛg Veda* and the ghosts of the *Atharva Veda* melted and coalesced under the powerful solvent of philosophy into the one supreme reality which, according to the qualities with which our imagination invests it, goes by this name or that.

The Epics relate the acceptance or new tribes and their gods into the old family circle. The clash of cults and the contact of cultures do not, as a rule, result in a complete domination of the one by the other. In all true contact there is an interchange of elements, though the foreign elements are given a new significance by those who accept them. The emotional attitudes attached to the old forms are transferred to the new which is fitted into the background of the old. Many tribes and races had mystic animals, and when the tribes entered the Hindu society the animals which followed them were made vehicles and companions of gods. One of them is mounted on the peacock, another on the swan, a third is carried by the bull,

[1] Many modern sects accept outsiders. Devala's smṛti lays down rules for the simple purification of people forcibly converted to other faiths, or of womenfolk defiled and confined for years, and even of people who, for worldly advantage, embrace other faiths.

and a fourth by the goat. The enlistment of Hanumān, the monkey-general, in the service of Rāma signifies the meeting-point of early nature worship and later theism. The dancing of Kṛṣṇa on Kālīya's head represents the subordination, if not the displacement, of serpent worship. Rāma's breaking of the bow of Śiva signifies the conflict between the Vedic ideal and the cult of Śiva, who soon became the god of the south (Dakṣiṇāmūrti). There are other stories in the Epic literature indicating the reconciliation of the Vedic and the non-Vedic faiths. The heroized ancestors, the local saints, the planetary influences and the tribal gods were admitted into the Hindu pantheon, though they were all subordinated to the one supreme reality of which they were regarded as aspects. The polytheism was organised in a monistic way. Only it was not a rigid monotheism enjoining on its adherents the most complete intolerance for those holding a different view.

It need not be thought that the Aryan was always the superior force. There are occasions when the Aryan yielded to the non-Aryan, and rightly too. The Epics relate the manner in which the different non-Aryan gods asserted their supremacy over the Aryan ones. Kṛṣṇa's struggle with Indra, the prince of the Vedic gods, is one instance. The rise of the cult of Siva is another. When Dakṣa, the protagonist of the sacrificial cult, conceives a violent feud against Śiva, there is disaffection in his own home, for his daughter Śati, who has become the embodiment of womanly piety and devotion, has developed an ardent love for Śiva.

The Vedic culture, which resembles that of the Homeric Greeks or the Celtic Irish at the beginning of the Christian era, or that of the pre-Christian Teutons and Slavs, becomes transformed in the Epics into the Hindu culture through the influence of the Dravidians. The Aryan idea of worship during the earliest period was to call on the Father Sky or some other shining one to look from on high on the sacrificer, and receive from him the offerings of fat or flesh, cakes and drink. But soon *pūjā* or worship takes the place of *homa* or sacrifice. Image worship which was a striking feature of the Dravidian faith was accepted by the Aryans. The ideals of vegetarianism and non-violence (*ahiṁsā*) also developed. The Vedic tradition was dominated by the Āgamic, and today Hindu culture shows the influence of the Āgamas, the sacred scriptures of the Jains, as much as that of the Vedas. The Aryan and the Dravidian do not exist side by side in Hinduism, but are worked up into a distinctive cultural pattern which is more an emergent than a resultant. The history of the Hindu religious development shows occasionally the friction between the two strains of the Vedas and the Āgamas, though they are sufficiently harmonized. When conceived in a large historical spirit, Hinduism becomes a slow growth across the centuries incorporating all the good and true things as well as much that is evil and erroneous, though a constant endeavour, which is not always successful, is kept up to throw out the unsatisfactory elements. Hinduism has the large comprehensive unity of a living organism with a fixed orientation. The Upaniṣad asks us to remember the Real who is One, who is indistinguishable through class or colour, and who by his varied forces provides as is necessary for the needs of each class and of all.

When once the cults are taken into Hinduism, alteration sets in as the result of the influence of the higher thought. The Hindu method of religious reform is essentially democratic. It allows each group to get to the truth through its own tradition by means of discipline of mind and morals. Each group has its own historic tradition, and assimilation of it is the condition of its growth of spirit. Even the savage clings to his superstitions obstinately and faithfully. For him his views are live forces, though they may seem to us no more than childish fancies. To shatter the superstitions of the savage is to destroy his morality, his social code and mental peace. Religious rites and social institutions, whatever they may be, issue out of experiences that may be hundreds of years old. As the Hindu inquirer cast his eyes over the manifold variety of the faiths which prevailed in his world, he saw that they were all conditioned by the social structure in which their followers lived. History has made them what they are, and they cannot be made different all of a sudden. Besides, God's gracious purpose includes the whole of the human race. Every community has inalienable rights which others should respect. No type can come into existence in which God does not live. Robert Burns truly says: 'And yet the light that led astray was light from heaven.' To despise other people's gods is to despise them, for they and their gods are adapted to each other. The Hindu took up the gods of even the savage and the uncivilized and set them on equal thrones to his own.

The right way to refine the crude beliefs of any group is to alter the bias of mind. For the view of God an individual stresses depends on the kind of man he is. The temperament and the training of the individual as well as the influence of the environment determine to a large extent the character of his religious opinions. Any defect in one's nature or onesidedness in one's experience is inevitably reflected in the view the individual adopts with regard to the religious reality. One's knowledge of God is limited by one's capacity to understand him. The aim of the reformer should be to cure the defect and not to criticize the view. When the spiritual life is quickened, the belief is altered automatically. Any change of view to be real must grow from within outwards. Opinions cannot grow unless traditions are altered. The task of the religious teacher is not so much to impose an opinion as to kindle an aspiration. If we open the eyes, the truth will be seen. The Hindu method adopts not force and threats but suggestion and persuasion. Error is only a sign of immaturity. It is not a grievous sin. Given time and patience it will be shaken off. However severe Hinduism may be with the strong in spirit, it is indulgent to the frailties of the weak.

The Hindu method of religious reform helps to bring about a change not in the name but in the content. While we are allowed to retain the same name, we are encouraged to deepen its significance. To take a familiar illustration, the Yahveh of the Pentateuch is a fearsome spirit, again and again flaming up in jealous wrath and commanding the slaughter of man, woman, child and beast, whenever his wrath is roused. The conception of the Holy One who loves mercy rather than sacrifice, who abominates burnt offerings, who reveals himself to those who yearn to know him asserts itself in the writings of Isaiah and Hosea. In the revelation of Jesus we have the conception of God as perfect love. The name 'Yahveh' is the common link which connects these different developments. When a new cult is accepted by Hinduism, the name is retained though a refinement of the content is effected. To take an example from early Sanskrit literature, it is clear that Kāli in her various shapes is a non-Aryan goddess.[1] But she was gradually identified with the supreme Godhead. Witness the following address to Kāli:

'Thou, O Goddess, O auspicious Remover of the distresses of those who turn to thee for refuge, art not to be known by speech, mind and intellect. None indeed is able to praise thee by words.

'O Goddess, having Brahman as thy personal form, O Mother of the universe, we repeatedly salute thee, full of compassion.

'The work of creation, maintenance and absorption is a mere wave of thy sportive pleasure. Thou art able to create the whole in a moment. Salutation to thee, O all-powerful Goddess! Although devoid of attributes and form, although standing outside of objective existence, although beyond the range of the senses, although one and whole and without a second and all-pervading, yet assuming a form possessed of attributes for the well-being of devotees, thou givest them the highest good. We salute thee, O Goddess, in whom all the three conditions of existence become manifest.'

Similarly Kṛṣṇa becomes the highest Godhead in the *Bhagavad-gītā* whatever his past origin may have been.

[1] In the *Mahābhārata* (iv. vii) we find that she delights in wine, flesh and animal sacrifices. *Gauḍavaho* (AD 700) refers to animal and human sacrifices offered to Kāli. Kṣudrakamalākara (fifteenth century AD), speaking of the image of Durgā at Vindhyachala near Mirzapur, says that Kāli is the goddess of the Kirātas and other aboriginal tribes and is worshipped by the Mlecchas, the Thugs, etc.

When the pupil approaches his religious teacher for guidance, the teacher asks the pupil about his favourite God, *iṣṭadevata*, for every man has a right to choose that form of belief and worship which most appeals to him. The teacher tells the pupil that his idea is a concrete representation of what is abstract, and leads him gradually to an appreciation of the Absolute intended by it. Suppose a Christian approaches a Hindu teacher for spiritual guidance, he would not ask his Christian pupil to discard his allegiance to Christ but would tell him that his idea of Christ was not adequate, and would lead him to a knowledge of the real Christ, the incorporate Supreme. Every God accepted by Hinduism is elevated and ultimately identified with the central Reality which is one with the deeper self of man. The addition of new gods to the Hindu pantheon does not endanger it. The critic who observes that Hinduism is 'magic tempered by metaphysics' or 'animism transformed by philosophy' is right. There is a distinction between magic tempered by metaphysics and pure magic. Hinduism absorbs everything that enters into it, magic or animism, and raises it to a higher level.

Differences in name become immaterial for the Hindu, since every name, at its best, connotes the same metaphysical and moral perfections. The identity of content signified by the different names is conveyed to the people at large by an identification of the names. Brahmā, Viṣṇu, Śiva, Kṛṣṇa, Kāli, Buddha and other historical names are used indiscriminately for the Absolute Reality. 'May Hari, the ruler of the three worlds worshipped by the Śaivites as Śiva, by the Vedāntins as Brahman, by the Buddhists as Buddha, by the Naiyāyikas as the chief agent, by the Jainas as the liberated, by the ritualists as the principle of law, may he grant our prayers.' Śaṁkara, the great philosopher, refers to the one Reality, who, owing to the diversity of intellects (*matibheda*) is conventionally spoken of (*parikalpya*) in various ways as Brahmā, Viṣṇu and Maheśvara.[1] A south Indian folksong says:

[1] *Haristuti*, 18.

# Hudsons University Bookshop

The New Refectory, The University, Birmingham B15 2TP
021-472 3034

*Our Ref:* U/VAMBLE/2 *Your Ref:* 4/3/81

We thank you for your recent order which we are unable to supply for the reason marked X below.

Radhakrishnan - East West in Religion

NOT YET PUBLISHED *order recorded*
BINDING—*copies expected shortly* *order recorded*
REPRINTING—*no date/expected* *weeks* *order recorded*
ON ORDER FROM U.S.A./EUROPE *order recorded*
NEW EDITION IN PREPARATION—
*no date/expected* *weeks* *order recorded*

X OUT OF PRINT—*order cancelled* ✓

*If undeivered please return to:*
Hudsons University Bookshop
The University
Edgbaston, Birmingham B15 2TP

Dr Ambler.
Theology Depr.

*Into the bosom of the one great sea*
*Flow streams that come from hills on every side,*
*Their names are various as their springs,*
*And thus in every land do men bow down*
*To one great God, though known by many names.*[2]

The Hindu method of reform enables every group to retain its past associations and preserve its individuality and interest. For as students are proud of their colleges, so are groups of their gods. We need not move students from one college to another, but should do our best to raise the tone of each college, improve its standards and refine its ideals, with the result that each college enables us to attain the same goal. It is a matter of indifference what college we are in, so long as all of them are steeped in the same atmosphere and train us to reach the same ideal. Of course there will be fanatics with narrow patriotism holding up Balliol as the best or Magdalene as modern, but to the impartial spectator the different colleges do not seem to be horizontal levels one higher than the other, but only vertical pathways leading to the same summit. We can be in any college and yet be on the lowest rung of the ladder or be high up in the scale. Where we are does not depend on the college but on ourselves. There are good Christians and bad Christians even as there are good Hindus and bad Hindus.

The Hindu method of reform has been criticized both from the theoretical and the practical points of view. Professor Clement Webb writes: 'With its traditions of periodically repeated incarnations of the deity in the most diverse forms, its ready acceptance of any and every local divinity or founder of a sect or ascetic devotee as a manifestation of God, its tolerance of symbols and legends of all kinds, however repulsive or obscene, by the side of the most exalted flights of world-renouncing mysticism, it could perhaps more easily than any other faith develop, without loss of continuity with its past, into a universal religion which would see in every creed a form, suited to some particular group or individual, of the

[2] Gover, *The Folksongs of Southern India* (1871), p. 165.

universal aspiration after one Eternal Reality, to whose true being the infinitely various shapes in which it reveals itself to, or conceals itself from men are all alike indifferent.'[1] While this statement represents the general tendency of the Hindu faith, it is not altogether fair to it when it suggests that for Hinduism there is nothing to choose between one revelation and another. Hinduism does not mistake tolerance for indifference. It affirms that while all revelations refer to reality, they are not equally true to it. Hinduism requires every man to think steadily on life's mystery until he reaches the highest revelation. While the lesser forms are tolerated in the interests of those who cannot suddenly transcend them, there is all through an insistence on the larger idea and the purer worship. Hinduism does not believe in forcing up the pace of development. When we give our higher experiences to those who cannot understand them we are in the position of those who can see and who impart the visual impressions to those born blind. Unless we open their spiritual eyes, they cannot see what the seers relate. So while Hinduism does not interfere with a man's natural way of thinking, which depends on his moral and intellectual gifts, education and environment, it furthers his spiritual growth by lending a sympathetic and helping hand wherever he stands. While Hinduism hates the compulsory conscription of men into the house of truth, it insists on the development of his intellectual conscience and sensibility to truth. Besides, error of judgment is not moral obliquity. Weakness of understanding is not depravity of heart. If a full and perfect understanding of the divine nature is necessary for salvation how many of us can escape the jaws of hell? *Śaktigītā* says: 'There is no limit, O Mother, to thy kindly grace in the case of devotees who are not able to realize thy form consisting of ideal essences, through the defects in the knowledge of principles.' We may not know God, but God certainly know us.

Hinduism has enough faith in the power of spirit to break the bonds that fetter the growth of the soul. God, the central reality affirmed by all religions, is the continual evolver of the

[1] Needham, *Science, Religion and Reality* (1926), pp. 334-5.

faiths in which men find themselves. Besides, experience proves that attempts at a very rapid progress from one set of rules to a higher one does not lead to advance but abrogation. The mills of the gods grind slowly in the making of history, and zealous reformers meet with defeat if they attempt to save the world in their own generation by forcing on it their favourite programmes. Human nature cannot be hurried. Again, Hinduism does not believe in bringing about a mechanical uniformity of belief and worship by a forcible elimination of all that is not in agreement with a particular creed. It does not believe in any statutory methods of salvation. Its scheme of salvation is not limited to those who hold a particular view of God's nature and worship. Such an exclusive absolutism is inconsistent with an all-loving universal God. It is not fair to God or man to assume that one people are the chosen of God, that their religion occupies a central place in the religious development of mankind, and that all others should borrow from them or suffer spiritual destitution.

After all, what counts is not creed but conduct. By their fruits ye shall know them and not by their beliefs. Religion is not correct belief but righteous living.[1] The truly religious never worry about other people's beliefs. Look at the great saying of Jesus: 'Other sheep I have which are not of this fold.' Jesus was born a Jew and died a Jew. He did not tell the Jewish people among whom he found himself, 'It is wicked to be Jews. Become Christians.' He did his best to rid the Jewish religion of its impurities. He would have done the same with Hinduism had he been born a Hindu. The true reformer purifies and enlarges the heritage of mankind and does not belittle, still less deny it.

Those who love their sects more than truth end by loving themselves more than their sects. We start by claiming that Christianity is the only true religion and then affirm that Protestantism is the only true sect of Christianity, Episcopalianism the only true Protestant Christian religion, and our

[1] Cp. Spinoza: 'Religion is universal to the human race; wherever justice and charity have the force of law and ordinance, there is God's kingdom.'

particular standpoint the only true representation of the High Church view.

The Hindu theory that every human being, every group and every nation has an individuality worthy of reverence is slowly gaining ground. Such a view requires that we should allow absolute freedom to every group to cultivate what is most distinctive and characteristic of it. All peculiarity is unique and incommunicable, and it will be to disregard the nature of reality to assume that what is useful to one will be useful to everyone else to the same extent. The world is wide enough to hold men whose natures are different.

It is argued sometimes that the Hindu plan has not helped its adherents to a freer and larger life. It is difficult to meet such an indefinite charge. Anyway, it is a matter of grave doubt whether Hinduism would have achieved a more effective regeneration if it had displaced by force the old ideas, i.e. if it had adopted the method of conversion and proselytism instead of reform resulting from gradual development. It is quite true that Hinduism did not cut away with an unsparing hand the rank tropical growth of magic and obscurantism. Its method is rather that of sapping the foundations than cutting the growths.

While in the great days of Hinduism there was a great improvement in the general religious life of the Hindus by the exercise of the two principles of respect for man and unbending devotion to truth, there has been a 'failure of nerve' in the Hindu spirit in recent times. There are within Hinduism large numbers who are the victims of superstition, but even in countries where the higher civilization is said to have displaced the lower, the lower still persists. To meet a savage we need not go very far. A great authority in these matters, Sir James Frazer, says: 'Among the ignorant and superstitious classes of modern Europe, it is very much what it was thousands of years ago in Egypt and India, and what it now is among the lowest savages surviving in the remotest corners of the world. Now and then the polite world is startled by a paragraph in a newspaper which tells how in Scotland an image has been found stuck full of pins for the purpose of killing an obnoxious laird or minister, how a woman has been slowly roasted to death as a witch in Ireland, or how a girl has been murdered and chopped up in Russia to make those candles of human tallow by whose light thieves hope to pursue their midnight trade unseen.'[1] Many Christians believe in spells and magic. Habits of human groups are hard to eradicate in proportion to the length of time during which they have existed. Rapid changes are impossible, and even slow changes are exceedingly difficult, for religions tend strongly to revert to type. When primitive tribes whose cults provided them with feminine as well as masculine objects of devotion entered the Buddhist fold they insisted on having in addition to the masculine Buddha the feminine Tārā. When the Græco-Romans worshiping Ashtoreth, Isis and Aphrodite entered the Christian Church, Mariolatry developed. It is related of an Indian Christian convert who attended the church on Sunday and the Kāli temple on Friday, that when the missionary gentleman asked him whether he was not a Christian, he replied, 'Yes, I am, but does it mean that I have changed my religion?' Hindu converts to other faiths frequently turn to Hindu gods in cases of trouble and sickness, presence or dread of death. Outer professions have no roots in inner life. We cannot alter suddenly our subconscious heritage at the bidding of the reformer. The old ideas cannot be rooted out unless we are educated to a higher intellectual and moral level.

The Hindu method has not been altogether a failure. There has been progress all round, though there is still room for considerable improvement. In spite of the fact that Hinduism has no common creed and its worship no fixed form, it has bound together multitudinous sects and devotions into a common scheme. In the Census Report for 1911 Mr Burns observes: 'The general result of my inquiries is that the great majority of Hindus have a firm belief in one supreme God, Bhagavān, Parameśvara, Īśvara, or Nārāyana.'[2] Regarding the spread of

[1] *The Golden Bough*, abridged edition (1922), p. 56.
[2] Part I, p. 362.

Hindu ideas and ideals, Sir Herbert Risley says: 'These ideas are not the monopoly of the learned, they are shared in great measure by the man in the street. If you talk to a fairly intelligent Hindu peasant about the Paramātmā, Karma, Māyā, Mukti, and so forth, you will find as soon as he has got over his surprise at your interest in such matters that the terms are familiar to him, and that he has formed a rough working theory of their bearing on his own future.'[1] There is an inner cohesion among the Hindus from the Himālayas to Cape Comorin.

The work of assimilating the rawest recruits of the hill-tribes and other half-civilized hordes has been a slow one and by no means thorough. Among Hindus are counted many professing crude beliefs and submerged thoughts which the civilization has not had time to eradicate. During the last few centuries Hinduism has not been faithful to its ideals, and the task of the uplift of the uncivilized has been sadly neglected.

Hinduism does not support the sophism that is often alleged that to coerce a man to have the right view is as legitimate as to save one by violence from committing suicide in a fit of delirium. The intolerance of narrow monotheism is written in letters of blood across the history of man from the time when first the tribes of Israel burst into the land of Canaan. The worshippers of the one jealous God are egged on to aggressive wars against people of alien cults. They invoke divine sanction for the cruelties inflicted on the conquered. The spirit of old Israel is inherited by Christianity and Islam, and it might not be unreasonable to suggest that it would have been better for Western civilization if Greece had moulded it on this question rather than Palestine. Wars of religion which are the outcome of fanaticism that prompts and justifies the extermination of aliens of different creeds were practically unknown in Hindu India. Of course, here and there there were outbursts of fanaticism, but Hinduism as a rule never encouraged persecution for unbelief. Its record has been a clean one, relatively

[1] *The People of India* (1915).

speaking. It has been able to hold together in peace many and varied communities of men. Buddhism, which counts among its followers nearly a fifth of the human race, has always respected other faiths and never tried to supplant them by force. One of the earliest Buddhist books relates that Buddha condemned the tendency prevalent among the religious disputants of his day, to make a display of their own doctrines and damn those of others.[1] Buddha asks his followers to avoid all discussions which are likely to stir up discontent among the different sects. Religious toleration is the theme of one of Aśoka's rock edicts, 'The King, beloved of the Gods, honours every form of religious faith, but considers no gift or honour so much as the increase of the substance of religion; whereof this is the root, to reverence one's own faith and never to revile that of others. Whoever acts differently injures his own religion while he wrong's another's.' 'The texts of all forms of religion shall be followed under my protection.'[2] The Hindu and the Buddhist rulers of India acted up to this principle with the result that the persecuted and the refugees of all great religions found shelter in India. The Jews, the Christians, the Parsees were allowed absolute freedom to develop on their own lines. Yuan Chwang reports that at the great festival of Prayāga, King Harṣa dedicated on the first day a statue to the Buddha, another to the sun, the favourite deity of his father, on the second, and to Śiva on the third. The famous Kottayam plates of Sthāṇuravi (ninth century AD) and the Cochin plates of Vijayarāgadeva bear eloquent testimony to the fact that the Hindu kings not only tolerated Christianity but granted special concessions to the professors of that faith. More recently, the Hindu prince of Mysore made a gift to the re-building of the Christian church in his State.

[1] *Sutta Nipāta*, 782; see also *Aṅguttara Nikāya*, iii. 57. 1, where Buddha encourages gifts by Buddhists to non-Buddhists as well. He admits the right of non-Buddhists to heaven. In the *Majjhima Nikāya* (i. p. 483) he mentions that a particular Ājīvaka gained heaven by virtue of his being a believer in Karma. Buddha held in high respect the Brahmins who led the truly moral life.

[2] The Twelfth Rock Edict.

Today the world has become a much smaller place, thanks to the adventures and miracles of science. Foreign nations have become our next-door neighbours. Mingling of populations is bringing about an interchange of thought. We are slowly realizing that the world is a single co-operative group. Other religions have become forces with which we have to reckon, and we are seeking for ways and means by which we can live together in peace and harmony. We cannot have religious unity and peace so long as we assert that we are in possession of the light and all others are groping in the darkness. That very assertion is a challenge to a fight. The political ideal of the world is not so much a single empire with a homogeneous civilization and a single communal will, but a brotherhood of free nations differing profoundly in life and mind, habits and institutions, existing side by side in peace and order, harmony and co-operation, and each contributing to the world its own unique and specific best, which is irreducible to the terms of the others. The cosmopolitanism of the eighteenth century and the nationalism of the nineteenth are combined in our ideal of a world-commonwealth, which allows every branch of the human family to find freedom, security and self-realization in the larger life of mankind. I see no hope for the religious future of the world, if this ideal is not extended to the religious sphere also. When two or three different systems claim that they contain the revelation of the very core and centre of truth and the acceptance of it is the exclusive pathway to heaven, conflicts are inevitable. In such conflicts one religion will not allow others to steal a march over it, and no one can gain ascendancy until the world is reduced to dust and ashes. To obliterate every other religion than one's own is a sort of bolshevism in religion which we must try to prevent. We can do so only if we accept something like the Hindu solution, which seeks the unity of religion not in a common creed but in a common quest. Let us believe in a unity of spirit and not of organization, a unity which secures ample liberty not only for every individual but for every type of organized life which has proved itself effective. For almost all historical forms of life and thought can claim the sanction of experience and so the authority of God. The world would be a much poorer thing if one creed absorbed the rest. God wills a rich harmony and not a colourless uniformity. The comprehensive and synthetic spirit of Hinduism has made it a mighty forest with a thousand waving arms each fulfilling its function and all directed by the spirit of God. Each thing in its place and all associated in the divine concert making with their various voices and even dissonances, as Heracletus would say, the most exquisite harmony should be our ideal.

That the Hindu solution of the problem of the conflict of religions is likely to be accepted in the future seems to me to be fairly certain. The spirit of democracy with its immense faith in the freedom to choose one's ends and direct one's course in the effort to realize them makes for it. Nothing is good which is not self-chosen; no determination is valuable which is not self-determination. The different religions are slowly learning to hold out hands of friendship to each other in every part of the world. The parliaments of religions and conferences and congresses of liberal thinkers of all creeds promote mutual understanding and harmony. The study of comparative religion is developing a fairer attitude to other religions. It is impressing on us the fundamental unity of all religions by pointing out that the genius of the people, the spirit of the age and the need of the hour determine the emphasis in each religion. We are learning to think clearly about the interrelations of religions. We tend to look upon different religions not as incompatibles but as complementaries, and so indispensable to each other for the realization of the common end. Closer contact with other religions has dispelled the belief that only this or that religion has produced men of courage and patience, self-denying love and creative energy. Every great religion has cured its followers of the swell of passion, the thrust of desire and the blindness of temper. The crudest religion seems to have its place in the cosmic scheme, for gorgeous flowers justify the muddy roots from which they spring. Growing insistence on mysticism is tending to a subordination of dogma.[1] While intellectualism would separate the dissimilar and shut them up in different compartments, higher intuition takes account of the natural differences of things and seeks to combine them in the ample unity of the whole. The half-religious and the irreligious fight about dogmas and not the truly religious. In the biting words of Swift, 'We have enough religion to hate one another but not enough to love one another.' The more religious we grow the more tolerant of diversity shall we become.

[1] Cp. Dean Inge: 'The centre of gravity in religion has shifted from authority to experience. . . . The fundamental principles of mystical religion are now very widely accepted, and are, especially with educated people, avowedly the main ground of belief.' *The Platonic Tradition in English Religious Thought* (1926), pp. 113-15.

CHAPTER III

# HINDU DHARMA: I

BEFORE we turn to the practical side of Hinduism, it is necessary to clear the ground by referring to some of the chief objections urged against the conception of Hindu ethics. The doctrine of *māyā* is supposed to repudiate the reality of the world and thus make all ethical relations meaningless. The world of nature is said to be unreal and human history illusory. There is no meaning in time and no significance in life. To be delivered from this illusion which has somehow come to dominate the race of man is the end of all endeavour.

The Vedic thinkers adopted a realistic view of the world. In the Upaniṣads we have an insistence on the relative reality of the world. The illustrations of a musical instrument and its notes, the substances of clay and gold and the things made of clay and gold, make out that the objects of the world derive their being from the Supreme. As Yājñavalkya puts it, everything in the world is of value as leading to the realization of self. When the *Śvetāśvatara Upaniṣad* looks upon the Supreme as the great Māyin, it suggests that this wonderful creation is his product. The Upaniṣads do not support the view that the Supreme calls up appearances which have no existence except in deluded minds. The different theistic systems adopted by the large majority of the Hindus do not advocate the doctrine of *māyā*. The theory is held by Śaṁkara, who is regarded often as representing the standard type of Hindu thought.

It is quite true that Śaṁkara regards the world as *māyā* and urges several reasons in support of his thesis. The manifold of experience whether of co-existence in space or sequence in time is ever incomplete and partial and we cannot unify it. There will always be a surplus uncovered by the largest unity.

The fact that the time and space world cannot be rounded into a systematic whole indicates that it is imperfect and unreal. Again, the real must be exempt from all change and persist for all time. The historical particulars do not persist for all time, they die every moment. We may interpret this idea in our own terms. The historical particular finishes its course when it reaches its end. If the end is not reached, if our lives are to be wasted in the pursuit of travelling perpetually and never arriving, then the world process is unmeaning and the cry that has gone forth that all is vanity becomes justified. It cannot be interminable singing, there should also be such a thing as completion in a song. If the historical process is not all, if we are not perpetually doomed to the pursuit of an unattainable ideal, then we must reach perfection at some point of the historical process, and that will be the transcending of our historical individuality, of our escape from birth and death, or saṁsāra. History is the working out of a purpose, and we are getting nearer and nearer to its fulfilment. *Mokṣa* is the realization of the purpose of each individual. On the attainment of perfection the historical existence terminates. When one individual completes his purpose, he develops the universality of outlook characteristic of perfection, but retains his individuality as a centre of action. When the whole universe reaches its consummation, the liberated individuals lapse into the stillness of the Absolute. Those great forces which seem to be making silently and surely for the destruction of this starry universe in which our earth swims as a speck will reach their true destination. The world fulfils itself by self-destruction. Einstein's theory of relativity with its assumption that the spatio-temporal system is limited and measurable is not unfavourable to such a dissolution of the world. But this does not take away from the free being of God who is omnipotence or infinite possibility. The curtain will drop on this world, but another possibility, another plot, another drama may commence and go on for ages.

To some it may appear that such a collapse of the world is a poor termination to all our struggles, and so they picture to us an eternal heaven or even eternal hell, but the implication of these eternal states is one of eternal idleness. As Herbert Spencer put it, deviation from perfection or the perfect adjustment of the organism to the environment is decay. The state of perfection is a condition of absolute stillness, stagnation, death. There are thinkers, both in the East and the West, who look upon Paradise as a state of activity where we sing the praises of God, and he has no end of patience in listening to his own glory. The only useful work which the liberated souls do is to help struggling humanity. So long as there are individuals who are unredeemed and so stand in need of saving knowledge, the liberated have some work to do. But if we allow that the world purpose is achieved, that all individuals have attained their perfection, there is nothing to be done. Aristotle says, 'Endless duration makes good no better, nor white any whiter.'[1] There is no creative process without travail, and the attainment of perfection for all means the end of creative activity. 'Nothing that is perfectly real moves', according to Bradley. Activity is a characteristic of the historical process, and perfection is not historical. It lacks nothing and it cannot have any activity in it.

It is sometimes argued that the world process is infinite and so there will always be work to be done. In other words, there will never come a time when all individuals will reach their perfection. But this will be a frustration of the purpose of God. So long as the world process continues, the liberated souls retain their individualities, which they lose in the event of the liberation of all, or *sarvamukti*.

It is not fair to represent Śaṁkara's view as an illusionism. Śaṁkara repudiates the subjectivism of Vijñānavādins and affirms the extra-mental reality of objects. His theory is not *dṛṣṭi-sṛṣṭi-vāda*, that objects rise into being when we perceive them and disappear when we do not. We perceive objects and do not simply contemplate apparitions. Śaṁkara distinguishes dreams from waking experiences and warns us against a confusion between the two. The experiences of waking life are not contradicted by anything else in our logical knowledge. He is a

[1] *Nicomachean Ethics*, i. 6.

realist so far as our experience goes. Things control thought. Śaṁkara's theory of *avidyā* also confirms this view. For *avidyā* is not a private profession of this or that individual mind; it is common to all minds, being the cosmic principle of finiteness. It is the cause of the whole empirical world (*pṛthivyādiprapañca*); common to all (*sarvasādhāraṇa*). *Mokṣa* or release of any one individual does not bring about the destruction of the world but only the displacement of a false outlook by a true one, *avidyā* by *vidyā*. When the illusion of the mirage is dissipated by scientific knowledge, the illusion stands there though it is no longer able to tempt us. The world is not so much denied as reinterpreted.

Śaṁkara believes that the logical dualism between subject and object is not final. It rests on a monism. Subject and object are phases of spirit. They have no existence apart from Brahman. 'There are in the world many universals with their particulars —both conscious and unconscious. All these universals in their graduated series are included and comprehended in one great universal, that is, Brahman as a mass of intelligence.'[1] Śaṁkara does not assert an identity between God and the world but only denies the independence of the world. As the Tīkākāra says: 'The world is not identical with Brahman; only it has no separate being independent of its ultimate source.' When Śaṁkara denies the reality of effects, he qualifies his denial by some such phrase as 'independent of the cause' or 'independent of God.'

If we raise the question as to how the finite rises from out of the bosom of the infinite, Śaṁkara says that it is an incomprehensible mystery, *māyā*. We know that there is the absolute reality, we know that there is the empirical world, we know that the empirical world rests on the Absolute, but the *how* of it is beyond our knowledge. The hypothesis of creation is a weak one, and it assumes that God lived alone for some time and then suddenly it occurred to him to have company, when he put forth the world. The theory of manifestation is not more satisfying, for it is difficult to know how the finite can manifest the

[1] Śaṁkara on *Bṛhadāraṇyakopaniṣad*, ii. 4. 9.

infinite. If we say that God is transformed into the world, the question arises whether it is the whole of God that is transformed or only a part. If it is the whole, then there is no God beyond the universe and we lapse into the lower pantheism. If it is only a part, then it means that God is capable of being partitioned. We cannot keep one part of God above and another part below. It would be like taking half a fowl for cooking, leaving the other half for laying eggs.[1] Śaṁkara believes that it is not possible to determine logically the relation between God and the world. He asks us to hold fast both ends. It does not matter if we are not able to find out where they meet.

The history of philosophy in India as well as Europe has been one long illustration of the inability of the human mind to solve the mystery of the relation of God to the world. The greatest thinkers are those who admit the mystery and comfort themselves by the idea that the human mind is not omniscient. Śaṁkara in the East and Bradley in the West adopt this wise attitude of agnosticism. We have the universe with its distinctions. It is not self-sufficient. It rests on something else, and that is the Absolute. The relation between the two is a mystery. The idea expressed in the statement 'And God saw everything that He had made and behold it was very good' does not solve the problem. It assumes that the world is 'very good' and we have our doubts about it. Unable to believe that a good God could be responsible for the horrors of nature, Plato held that the goodness of God was made somewhat ineffective by the intractableness of nature which he tried in vain to control. The Gnostics strove to express the idea that God was trying to redeem a world created by the devil. Augustine from this worked our his view of 'total depravity' and the scheme of salvation. Some still clung to the idea of the omnipotence of God by paying him the doubtful compliment, as J. S. Mill says, of making him the creator of the devil. Leibniz argues that even if this world is in many ways defective, it is the best of all possible worlds; but this view implies an uncomplimentary reflection on the power of God. Hegelian absolutism is unable

[1] Ānandagiri on *Brahma Sūtra*, i. 2-8.

to account for the lapse of the perfect into the imperfect. Bergson emphasizes the conflict of matter and life in the world and believes that the two are the negative and positive phases of one primal consciousness, but he is not able to account for the rise of the two tendencies from the first principle. Croce arrives at the different forms of spirit, theoretical and practical, but he does not give us any metaphysical deduction of these forms from the one spirit. If the forms are all, then there is no Absolute, and if there is no Absolute, it seems to be a sort of dissolute Absolute.

A wise agnosticism is more faithful to the situation. But the logical mind of man is not willing to admit defeat. It cannot rest in the idea that the Absolute is incomprehensible and that the world hangs on it somehow. It makes the Absolute determinate and relates the world to this determinate principle as its expression. In view of the weakness of the human mind Śaṁkara allows these metaphors. The perfection of God overflows into the world. The world is the outflow of the surplus energies of God, the supreme artist. *Līlā* or sport brings out the rationality, the freedom and the joyous exercise of spontaneity involved in the art of creation. We look upon God as a personal lord, and endow him with the power of self-expression and self-communication. A sterile perfection is an inconceivability. The principle of self-expression is also called *māyā*. It also stands for the principle of objectivity by interaction with which the subject self is able to express himself. But these attempts are devices to understand the nature of the relation of God to the world.

However that may be, no theory has ever asserted that life is a dream and all experienced events are illusions. One or two later followers of Śaṁkara lend countenance to this hypothesis, but it cannot be regarded as representing the main tendency of Hindu thought.

The next objection goes to the opposite extreme. To the Hindu ethical rules are meaningless because the world is divine. Everything is God, and there is no excuse for our interfering with the sacred activities of the pickpocket and the perjurer. The critic believes that he refutes the theory of divine immanence associated with all forms of Indian thought when he exclaims, Is Piccadilly Circus God? is Hyde Park Corner God? The Hindu view rebels against the cold and formal conception of God who is external to the world, and altogether remote and transcendent. The natural law of the world is but a working of God's sovereign purpose The uniformity of nature, the orderliness of the cosmos, and the steady reaching forward and upward of the course of evolution proclaim not the unconscious throbbing of a soulless engine, but the directing mind of an all-knowing spirit. The indwelling of God in the universe does not mean the identity of God with the universe. According to the latter view God is so immanent in everything that we have only to open our eyes to see God in it, but also there is nothing of God left outside the whole of things. God lies spread out before us. The world is not only a revelation, but an exhaustive revelation of God. Hindu thought takes care to emphasize the transcendent character of the Supreme. 'He bears the world but is by no means lost in it.' The world is in God and not God in the world. In the universe we have the separate existence of the individuals. Whether the divine spark burns dimly or brightly in the individual, the sparks are distinct from the central fire from which they issue.

Hindu thought admits that the immanence of God is a fact admitting of various degrees. While there is nothing which is not lit by God, God is more fully revealed in the organic than in the inorganic, more in the conscious than in the unconscious, more in man than in the lower creatures, more in the good man than in the evil. But even the worst of the world cannot be dismissed as completely undivine, fit only to be cast into hell fire. While Hinduism believes in the divine indwelling and declares that there is no escaping from the divine presence, it does not say that everything is God as we find it. Piccadilly is not God, though even Piccadilly cannot be unless it is allowed by divine activity. There are divine potentialities in even the worst of men, the everlasting arms of God underneath the worst sinners. No one is really beyond hope. The worst sinner has a future even as the greatest saint has had a past. No one is so good or so bad as he imagines. The great souls of the world address themselves to the task of rousing the divine possibilities in the publicans and the sinners.

The doctrine of Karma is sometimes interpreted as implying a denial of human freedom, which is generally regarded as the basis of all ethical values. But when rightly viewed the law does not conflict with the reality of freedom. It is the principle of science which displaces belief in magic or the theory that we can manipulate the forces of the world at our pleasure. The course of nature is determined not by the passions and prejudices of personal spirits lurking behind it but by the operation of immutable laws. If the sun pursues his daily and the moon her nightly journey across the sky, if the silent procession of the seasons moves in light and shadow across the earth, it is because they are all guided in their courses by a power superior to them all. 'Verily O Gārgī, at the command of that Imperishable, the sun and the moon stand apart, the earth and the sky stand apart . . . the moments, the hours, the days, the nights, the fortnights, the months, the seasons and the years stand apart. Verily O Gārgī, at the command of that Imperishable, some rivers flow from the snowy mountains to the east, others to the west in whatever direction each flows.'[1] There is the march of necessity everywhere. The universe is lawful to the core.

The theory of Karma recognizes the rule of law not only in outward nature, but also in the world of mind and morals. *Ṛta* manifests itself equally in nature and in human society. We are every moment making our characters and shaping our destinies. 'There is no loss of any activity which we commence nor is there any obstacle to its fulfilment. Even a little good that we may do will protect us against great odds.'[2] What we have set our hearts on will not perish with this body. This fact inspires life with the present sense of eternity.

At a time when people were doing devil's work under divine sanction and consoling themselves by attributing everything

[1] *Bṛh. Up.*, iii. 8. 9.
[2] *Bhagavadgītā*, iii. 40.

to God's will, the principle of Karma insisted on the primacy of the ethical and identified God with the rule of law. All's law, yet all's God. Karma is not a mechanical principle but a spiritual necessity. It is the embodiment of the mind and will of of God. God is its supervisor, *karmādhyakṣaḥ*.[1] Justice is an attribute of God. Character of God is represented by St James as one 'with whom can be no variation neither shadow that is cast by turning'. Every act, every thought is weighed in the invisible but universal balance-scales of justice. The day of judgment is not in some remote future, but here and now, and none can escape it. Divine laws cannot be evaded. They are not so much imposed from without as wrought into our natures. Sin is not so much a defiance of God as a denial of soul, not so much a violation of law as a betrayal of self. We carry with us the whole of our past. It is an ineffaceable record which time cannot blur nor death erase.

There is room for repentance and consequent forgiveness on this scheme. The critic who urges that belief in Karma makes religious life, prayer and worship impossible has not a right understanding of it. In his opinion God has abdicated in favour of his law. To pray to God is as futile a superstition as to bid the storm give us strength, or the earthquake to forgive us our sins. Of course the Hindu does not look upon prayer as a sort of Aladdin's lamp to produce anything we want. God is not a magician stopping the sun in its course and staying the bullet in its march. But his truth and constancy, his mercy and justice find their embodiment in the implacable working of the moral law. Forgiveness is not a mitigation of God's justice but only an expression of it. We can insist with unflinching rigour on the inexorability of the moral law and yet believe in the forgiveness of sins. Spiritual growth and experience are governed by laws similar to those which rule the rest of the universe. If we sow to the flesh we shall of the flesh reap corruption. The punishment for a desecrated body is an enfeebled understanding and a darkened soul. If we deliberately fall into sin, shutting our eyes to moral and spiritual light, we may be sure that in

[1] *Śvet. Up.*, vi. 11.

God's world sin will find us out and our wilful blindness will land us in the ditch. A just God cannot refuse to any man that which he has earned. The past guilt cannot be wiped away by the atoning suffering of an outward substitute.[1] Guilt cannot be transferred. It must be atoned for through the sorrow entailed by self-conquest. God cannot be bought over and sin cannot be glossed over.

The principle of Karma reckons with the material or the context in which each individual is born. While it regards the past as determined, it allows that the future is only conditioned. The spiritual element in man allows him freedom within the limits of his nature. Man is not a mere mechanism of instincts. The spirit in him can triumph over the automatic forces that try to enslave him. The *Bhagavadgītā* asks us to raise the self by the self. We can use the material with which we are endowed to promote our ideals. The cards in the game of life are given to us. We do not select them. They are traced to our past Karma, but we can call as we please, lead what suit we will, and as we play, we gain or lose. And there is freedom.

What the individual will be cannot be predicted beforehand, though there is no caprice. We can predict an individual's acts so far as they are governed by habit, that is, to the extent his actions are mechanical and not affected by choice. But choice is not caprice. Free will in the sense of an undetermined, unrelated, uncaused factor in human action is not admitted, but such a will defies all analysis. It has nothing to do with the general stream of cause and effect. It operates in an irregular and chaotic way. If human actions are determined by such a will, there is no meaning in punishment or training of character. The theory of Karma allows man the freedom to use the material in the light of his knowledge. Man controls the uniformities in nature, his own mind and society. There is thus scope for genuine rational freedom, while indeterminism and chance lead to a false fatalism.

The universe is not one in which every detail is decreed. We

[1] Cp. munir manute mūrkho mucyate. The monk meditates and the fool is freed.

do not have a mere unfolding of a pre-arranged plan. There is no such thing as absolute prescience on the part of God, for we are all his fellow-workers. God is not somewhere above us and beyond us, he is also in us. The divine in us can, if utilized, bring about even sudden conversions. Evolution in the sense of epigenesis is not impossible. For the real is an active developing life and not a mechanical routine.

The law of Karma encourages the sinner that it is never too late to mend. It does not shut the gates of hope against despair and suffering, guilt and peril. It persuades us to adopt a charitable view towards the sinner, for men are more often weak than vicious. It is not true that the heart of man is desperately wicked and that he prefers evil to good, the easy descent to hell to the steep ascent to heaven.

Unfortunately, the theory of Karma became confused with fatality in India when man himself grew feeble and was disinclined to do his best. It was made into an excuse for inertia and timidity and was turned into a message of despair and not of hope. It said to the sinner, 'Not only are you a wreck, but that is all you ever could have been. That was your preordained being from the beginning of time.' But such a philosophy of despair is by no means the necessary outcome of the doctrine of Karma.

Let us now turn to the practical side of Hinduism. Hinduism is more a way of life than a form of thought. While it gives absolute liberty in the world of thought it enjoins a strict code of practice. The theist and the atheist, the sceptic and the agnostic may all be Hindus if they accept the Hindu system of culture and life. Hinduism insists not on religious conformity but on a spiritual and ethical outlook in life. 'The performer of the good—and not the believer in this or that view—can never get into an evil state'.[1] In a very real sense practice precedes theory. Only by doing the will does one know the doctrine. Whatever our theological beliefs and metaphysical opinions may be, we are all agreed that we should be kind and honest, grateful to our benefactors and sympathetic to the unfortunate.

[1] *Bhagavadgītā*, vii. 40.

Hinduism insists on a moral life and draws into fellowship all who feel themselves bound to the claims which the moral law makes upon them. Hinduism is not a sect but a fellowship of all who accept the law of right and earnestly seek for the truth.

Dharma is right action. In the *Ṛg Veda*, *ṛta* is the right order of the universe. It stands for both the *satya* or the truth of things as well as the dharma or the law of evolution. Dharma formed from the root *dhṛ*, to hold, means that which holds a thing and maintains it in being. Every form of life, every group of men has its dharma, which is the law of its being. Dharma or virtue is conformity with the truth of things; adharma or vice is opposition to it. Moral evil is disharmony with the truth which encompasses and controls the world.

Desires constitute the springs of human action. The life of man centres round certain basic cravings, each distinct from the other in its object and each stimulating men to a particular mode of activity in order to satisfy it. If the several desires were independent of one another and never crossed or modified one another, then their different expressions would be separate and unco-ordinated. Family life will have little to do with economic pursuits. Industrial relations will be ethically colourless. Religious activities may be indifferent to the secular sides of life. But man is a whole, and so all his activites have an overarching unity. Each individual has in him the sex and the parental instincts, love of power and wealth, desire for the common good and a hunger for communion with the unseen. These different activites react upon and modify one another. They function in interdependence in man's life. If life is one, then there is one master science of life which recognizes the four supreme ends of *dharma* or righteousness, *artha* or wealth, *kāma* or artistic and cultural life, and *mokṣa* or spiritual freedom. The Hindu code of practice links up the realm of desires with the perspective of the eternal. It binds together the kingdoms of earth and heaven.

Hinduism does not believe in any permanent feud between the human world of natural desires and social aims and the spiritual life with its discipline and aspiration on the other. It condemns only natural existence which is unrelated to the background. Such a life which concentrates on this world and its good things is not satisfying, for the greatest prosperity comes to its end, dissolving into emptiness. The world and all else on which we pin our faith will desert us in the moment of our triumph. The Hindu thinker dwells on the evanescence of the world and its pitiful futility if its connection with the eternal is snapped.

All worldly relationships have their end, but they cannot be ignored. To behave as if they do not exist simply because they do not persist is to court disaster. The eternal is manifested in the temporal, and the latter is the pathway to the former. Truth in the finite aspect leads us to infinite truth. Renunciation is the feeling of detachment from the finite as finite and attachment to the finite as the embodiment of the infinite. The two are bound to each other and to separate them is ruinous. The Upaniṣad says: 'In darkness are they who worship only the world, but in greater darkness they who worship the infinite alone. He who accepts both saves himself from death by the knowledge of the former and attains immortality by the knowledge of the latter.'

*Artha* takes note of the economic and the political life of man, the craving for power and property. The urge which gives rise to property is something fundamental in human nature. Unless we change the constitution of the human mind, we cannot eradicate the idea of property. For most men property is the medium for the expression of personality and intercourse with others.

While the pursuit of wealth and happiness is a legitimate human aspiration, they should be gained in ways of righteousness (*dharma*), if they are to lead ultimately to the spiritual freedom of man (*mokṣa*). Each one of these ends requires ethical discipline. Freedom can be obtained only through bonds of discipline and surrender of personal inclination. To secure the freedom to acquire and to enjoy we have to limit ourselves and bind our will in certain ways. The countries which are politically free are largely bound in thought and practice. Political freedom is not possible without a large curtailment of freedom of thought and action. In the interests of spiritual freedom Hindu society regulated the most intimate details of daily life, and they are the rules of dharma. These rules are not the same in all parts of the country or in all periods of Hindu history. The Hindu legislators accepted the bewildering variety of customs professed by the tribes in India as the civilization spread from the Indus to the Cape. The law books recognize the variety, though they try to refine whatever seems to be morally objectionable.[1] While recognizing them all an ideal standard is enjoined which imperceptibly brings about a refinement of the customs. According to the *Taittirīya Upaniṣad*, the young man is asked in cases of doubt to take as his authority what is done in similar circumstances by the Brahmins 'competent to judge, apt and devoted but not harsh, lovers of virtue.' Manu urges that the conduct of good people (*sadbhiḥ*) and righteous souls of the regenerate classes (*dhārmikaiś ca dvijātibhiḥ*) may be regarded as consistent (*aviruddham*) with the customs of all countries, familes and castes.

*Mokṣa* is spiritual realization. The Hindu Dharma says, Man does not live by bread alone, nor by his work, capital, ambition or power or relations to external nature. He lives or must live by his life of spirit. *Mokṣa* is self-emancipation, the fulfilment of the spirit in us in the heart of the eternal. This is what gives ultimate satisfaction, and all other activities are directed to the realization of this end.

As to the methods of obtaining freedom, the Hindu thinker adopted a very catholic attitude. 'As the birds fly in the air, as the fish swim in the sea, leaving no traces behind, even so is the pathway to God traversed by the seeker of spirit.'

The different pathways have been broadly distinguished into the three types of *jñāna*, wisdom, *bhakti* or devotion, *karma* or service. The three are not exclusive, but emphasize the dominant aspects. Wisdom (*jñāna*) does not mean intellectual

[1] See Baudhāyana, Bṛhaspati, Devala, Gautama.

acumen or dialectical power. *Jñāna* is realized experience. We are saved from sin only when we live in the presence of God. If we have true insight, right action will take care of itself. Truth cannot but act rightly. The way of devotion is the most popular one. Sinners as well as saints, ignorant as well as learned, foolish as well as wise find it easy. Prayer and petition, fasting and sacrifice, communion and self-examination, all are included in the life of devotion. In its highest flights, *bhakti* coincides with *jñāna*, and both these issue in right *karma* or virtuous life.

While the individual and the social sides of karma are inseparably intertwined, the theory of *varṇa* or caste emphasizes the social aspect, and that of *āśrama* or stages of life the individual aspect. The four stages of *brahmacarya* or the period of training, *gārhastya* or the period of work for the world as a householder, *vānaprasthya* or the period of retreat for the loosening of the social bonds, and *samnyāsa* or the period of renunciation and expectant awaiting of freedom indicate that life is a pilgrimage to the eternal life through different stages.

The first period is that of training and discipline of body and mind. Plastic youth is moulded to a life of duty. The student is required to live for a fixed period in the house of his teacher, where he is taught the arts and sciences which would be useful to him in after life. Women were also entitled to *brahmacarya*. They were given the training of their classes, and thus enabled to take up the functions of the caste in the emergencies of life. Restrictions regarding Vedic study were introduced when women of other racial stocks with different customs were accepted in marriage.

The second stage is that of the householder or the *gṛhastha*. A human being is not ordinarily self-sufficing. The God of Aristotle may enjoy his solitary existence, but not the men and women of the world. These are as a rule encouraged to enter the married life.[1] India has known for centuries what Freud

[1] According to *Harita Smṛti* (xx. 23), quoted by Sāyaṇa in his commentary on *Parāśara Saṁhitā* (Bombay Sanskrit Series, Part II, p. 82), girls are divided into two classes: Brahmavādinīs, or those who are devoted to sacred wisdom, and Sadyovadhūs, or those who get married. Some of the well-known women

is popularizing in Europe, that repressed desires are more corrupting in their effects than those exercised openly and freely. Monastic tendencies were discouraged until one had a normal expression of natural impulses. He who runs back from marriage is in the same boat with one who runs away from battle. Only failures in life avoid occasions for virtue. Marriage is regarded as sacred. The very gods are married. When the Hindu descends from the adoration of the Absolute and takes to the worship of a personal god, his god has always a consort. He does not worship a bachelor or a virgin. Śiva is *ardhanārīśvara*, and his image signifies the co-operative interdependent, separately incomplete but jointly complete masculine and feminine functions of the supreme being. There is nothing unwholesome or guilty about the sex life. Through the institution of marriage it is made the basis of intellectual and moral intimacies. Marriage is not so much a concession to human weakness as a means of spiritual growth. It is prescribed for the sake of the development of personality as well as the continuance of the family ideal. Marriage has this social side. Every family is a partnership between the living and the dead. The Śrāddha ceremony is intended to impress the idea of the family solidarity on the members. At the end of the ceremony the performer asks, 'Let me, O fathers! have a hero for a son.'[1]

The Hindu ideal emphasizes the individual and the social aspects of the institution of marriage. Man is not a tyrant nor is woman a slave, but both are servants of a higher ideal to which their individual inclinations are to be subordinated. Sensual love is sublimated into self-forgetful devotion. Marriage for the Hindu is a problem and not a datum. Except in the pages of fiction we do not have a pair agreeing with each other in everything, tastes and temper, ideals and interests. Irreducible peculiarities there will always be, and the task of

---

of early Sanskrit literature, like Gārgī in the *Bṛh. Up.*, Sulabhā in *Mahābharata*, Śabarī in the *Rāmāyaṇa*, lived unmarried lives. The Hindu social code deals not so much with such exceptional cases as with the typical course and its functional rule. It legislates for the normal.

[1] Cp. the Vedic prayer, May we have great heroes amongst us.

the institution of marriage is to use these differences to promote a harmonious life. Instincts and passions are the raw material which are to be worked up into an ideal whole. Though there is some choice with regard to our mates, there is a large element of chance in the best of marriages. Carve as we will that mysterious block of which our life is made, the black vein of destiny or chance, whatever we may call it, appears again and again in it. That marriage is successful which transforms a chance mate into a life companion. Marriage is not the end of the struggle, it is but the beginning of a strenuous life where we attempt to realize a larger ideal by subordinating our private interests and inclinations. Service of a common ideal can bind together the most unlike individuals. Love demands its sacrifices. By restraint and endurance, we raise love to the likeness of the divine.

In an ideal marriage the genuine interests of the two members are perfectly reconciled. The perfectly ethical marriage is the monogamous one. The relation of Rāma and Sītā, or Sāvitrī and Satyavān, where the two stand by each other against the whole world, is idealized in the Hindu scriptures. In the absence of absolute perfection we have to be content with approximations. We need not, however, confound the higher with the lower. Eight different kinds of marriages are recognized in the Hindu law books. Manu did not shut his eyes to the practices of his contemporaries. He arranges the different kinds of marriages in an order. While marriages in which personal inclination is subordinated rank high, those by mutual choice (*gāndharva*), force (*rākṣasa*), purchase (*āsura*) come lower. The lowest is *paiśāca*. When the lover ravishes a maiden without her consent, when she is asleep, or intoxicated or deranged in mind, we have a case of *paiṣāca* marriage.[1] It is a very low kind of marriage, but admitted as valid with the laudable motives of giving the injured women the status of wives and their offspring legitimacy.

Insistence on the interests of the family led to a compromise of the monogamous ideal. While the monogamous ideal is

[1] *Manu*, iii. 34.

held up as the best, polygamy was also tolerated. When you have no male offspring, or when, by mistake or chance, you seduce a woman when you are married, it is your duty to protect her from desertion and from public scorn, save her from a life of infamy and degradation, and protect her children who are in no way responsible for the ways of their parents; in such cases polygamy is permissible. The story of the epic Rāmāyana has for one of its chief lessons the evils of polygamy. The palace of Daśaratha was a centre of intrigue, and Rāma, the hero of the story, stands up for the monogamous ideal.

A system which looks upon marriage as compulsory for all has its own weaknesses, though it does not develop large numbers of unmarried women who see no meaning in life. It is obliged to discountenance the remarriage of widows.[1] It unconsciously tends to lower the marriageable age of girls. It is necessary for the leaders to remember the Hindu ideals and bring about a more satisfactory state of affairs.

The recognition of the spiritual ideal of marriage requires us to regard the marriage relation as an indissoluble one. So long as we take a small view of life and adopt for our guide the fancy or feeling of the moment, marriage relation cannot be regarded as permanent. In the first moments of infatuation we look upon our partners as angels from heaven, but soon the wonder wears away, and if we persist in our passion for perfection, we become agitated and often bitter. The unrest is the effect of a false ideal. The perfect relation is to be created and not found. The existence of incompatibility is a challenge to a more vigorous effort. To resort to divorce is to confess defeat. The misfits and the maladjustments are but failures.

Modern conditions are responsible for the large numbers of divorces and separations. Life has become too hurried. We have no time to understand one another. To justify our conduct, we are setting up exaggerated claims on behalf of the individual will and are strongly protesting against discipline. We are confusing self-expression and self-development with a life of instincts and passions. We tend to look upon ourselves as

[1] But see *Ṛg Veda*, x. 18. 8; *Āśvalāyana*, iv. 2. 18; *Agni Purāṇa*, cliii.

healthy animals and not spiritual beings. We have had sin with us from the beginning of our history, but we have recently begun to worship it. It is not very modern for a man or woman who is sick of his or her partner to take to another, but what is really modern is the new philosophy in justification of it. Disguised feeling is masquerading as advanced thought. The woman who gives up her husband for another is idealized as a heroine who has had the courage to give up the hypocritical moral codes and false sentiments, while she who clings to her husband through good report and bad is a cowardly victim of conventions. Sex irregularities are becoming less shocking and more popular.

Though we have had our share of exaggerating the wickedness of women, and though we have some texts which regard the woman as the eternal temptress of the man Adam, a snare of perdition, as Donaldson expressed it, 'a fireship continually striving to get alongside the male man-of-war and blow him up into pieces', the general Hindu view of woman is an exalted one. It regards the woman as the helpmate of man in all his work, *sahadharmiṇī*.[1] The Hindu believes in the speciality of the contribution which woman makes to the world. She has special responsibilities and special duties. Even such an advanced thinker as Mrs Bertrand Russell allows that 'each class and sex has that to give to the common stock of achievement, knowledge and thought which it alone can give, and robs itself and the community by inferior imitation'.[2] So long as children cannot be shaken from heaven, but have to be built within their mothers' bodies, so long will there be a specific function for women. As the bearing and rearing of children take a good deal of their time and attention, women were relieved of the economic responsibilities for the family. While man is expected to take to the worldly pursuits (*yajñaprādhānya*), woman is capable of great heights of self-control and self-denial (*tapaḥ-*

[1] Sāyaṇa, commenting on *Ṛg Veda*, v. 61. 8, says: 'The wife and the husband, being the equal halves of one substance, are equal in every respect; both should join and take equal part in all work, religious and secular.' This ideal is lowered in some passages of *Manu* and *Yājñavalkya*.

[2] *Hypatia* (1925).

*prādhānya*). The stricter code of morality applied to women is really a compliment to them, for it accepts the natural superiority of the women. But the modern woman, if I may say so, is losing her self-respect. She does not respect her own individuality and uniqueness, but is paying an unconscious tribute to man by trying to imitate him. She is fast becoming masculine and mechanical. Adventurous pursuits are leading her into conflict with her own inner nature.

The third stage arises when the responsibilities of home are given up. The wife accompanies the husband to the forest, if she shares his spiritual aims. According to Manu, one must enter the third stage when one becomes a grandfather, or one's skin begins to show wrinkles or one's hair turns grey. When one's bodily powers wane, it is time to depart to the forest and prepare oneself for the true life of the spirit. The main objective of this stage is to escape from the bustle of life into the solitude of the forest to meditate on the higher problems.

The stature of man is not to be reduced to the requirements of the society. Man is much more than the custodian of its culture or protector of his country or producer of its wealth. His social efficiency is not the measure of his spiritual manhood. The soul which is our spiritual life contains our infinity within it. What shall it profit a man if he gain the whole world but lose his own soul? A Sanskrit verse reads: 'For the family sacrifice the individual; for the community the family; for the country the community, and for the soul the whole world.' Family and country, nation and the world cannot satisfy the soul in man. Each individual is called upon at a certain stage of his life to give up his wife and children and his caste and work. The last part of life's road has to be walked in single file.

The aim of the *samnyāsin* is not to free himself from the cares of outward life, but to attain a state of spiritual freedom when he is not tempted by riches or honour, and is not elated by success or depressed by failure. He develops a spirit of equanimity and so 'bears patiently improper words and does not insult anyone; he does not hate anyone for the sake of his physical body'.[1] These free men are solitary souls who have not any personal attachments or private ambitions, but embody in their own spirit the freedom of the world. They take on the wideness of the whole earth, dwell in love and walk in righteousness. The social order regards the *samnyāsin* as a parasite since he does not contribute to it materially and does not care for its forms. The state looks on him with suspicion as he does not profess any loyalty to any family or church, race or nation. He does not function in any industrial factory, social system or political machine. These *samnyāsins* do not serve our policies that make the world unsafe for human life, do not promote our industries that mechanize persons, and do not support our national egoisms that provoke wars. Patriotism is not enough for these fine souls. Life, and not India's life or England's life, demands their devotion. They look upon all men and all groups as equal (*samatā sarvasmin*).

While some forms of Christianity and Buddhism judge the life of the world to be inferior to the life of the monk, and would have loved to place the whole of mankind at one swoop in the cloister, Hinduism while appreciating the life of the *samnyāsin* refrained from condemning the state of the householder. Every state is necessary, and in so far as it is necessary it is good. The blossom does not deny the leaf and the leaf does not deny the stalk nor the stalk the root. The general rule is that we should pass from stage to stage gradually.

The liberated soul is not indifferent to the welfare of the world. Renunciation is the surrendering of the notions of I and mine, and not the giving up of the work enjoined by the scriptures. It is related of the Buddha that when he was on the threshold of nirvāṇa he turned away and took the vow never to cross it so long as a single being remained subject to sorrow and suffering. The same idea comes out in the sublime verse of the *Bhāgavata*: 'I desire not the supreme state (of bliss) with its eight perfections, nor the cessation of rebirth. May I take up the sorrow of all creatures who suffer and enter into them so that they may be made free from grief.' Mahādeva the prince

[1] *Manu*, vi. 47 ff.

of ascetics drank poison for the sake of the world. Freedom on the highest level of existence expresses itself on the lower as courage to suffer, sacrifice, and die.

This fourfold plan of life yet dominates the Hindu mind. The general character of a society is not always best expressed by the mass of its members. There exists in every community a natural élite, which better than all the rest represents the soul of the entire people, its great ideals, its strong emotions and its essential tendency. The whole community looks to them as their example. When the wick is ablaze at its tip, the whole lamp is said to be burning.

CHAPTER IV

# HINDU DHARMA: II

THE institution of caste illustrates the spirit of comprehensive synthesis characteristic of the Hindu mind with its faith in the collaboration of races and the co-operation of cultures. Paradoxical as it may seem, the system of caste is the outcome of tolerance and trust. Though it has now degenerated into an instrument of oppression and intolerance, though it tends to perpetuate inequality and develop the spirit of exclusiveness, these unfortunate effects are not the central motives of the system. If the progressive thinkers of India had the power, as they undoubtedly have the authority, they would transform the institution out of recognition. It is not the evils of the system that I am here concerned with so much as the underlying principles.

Any survey of the castes of the present day will reveal the complex origin of the institution. Castes are of many kinds, tribal, racial, sectarian, occupational. Some are due to migration. When members of an old caste migrate to a different part of the country, they become a new caste.

As it is clear from the Sanskrit word *varṇa*, caste had originally reference to colour. If we look into the past history of India, we see how the country has been subjected to one race invasion after another. Even at the beginning of her history India was peopled by various racial groups, the dark aboriginal tribes, the sturdy Dravidians, the yellow-skinned Mongols and the blithe, forceful Aryans. Very soon she developed intimate intercourse with the Persians, the Greeks and the Scythians, and some of these settled down in India. No other country in the world has had such racial problems as India.

Regarding the solution of the problem of racial conflicts the different alternatives which present themselves are those of extermination, subordination, identification or harmonization. The first course has been adopted often in the course of the history of the world. The trail of man is dotted with the graves of countless communities which reached an untimely end. But is there any justification for this violation of human life? Have we any idea of what the world loses when one racial culture is extinguished? It is true that the Red Indians have not made, to all appearance, any contribution to the world's progress, but have we any clear understanding of their undeveloped possibilities which, in God's good time, might have come to fruition? Do we know so much of ourselves and the world and God's purpose as to believe that our civilization, our institutions and our customs are so immeasurably superior to those of others, not only what others actually possess but what exists in them potentially? We cannot measure beforehand the possibilities of a race. Civilizations are not made in a day, and had the fates been kindlier and we less arrogant in our ignorance, the world, I dare say, would have been richer for the contributions of the Red Indians. Our civilization is quite recent when compared with the antiquity of man and the differentiation of human types. Some of the ancestors of the Great British people who are now in the vanguard of humanity were not much advanced as depicted by Julius Cæsar. Who could understand the great potentialities of the savages of Britain dressed in skins at their religious worship burning men alive to appease their gods? No one acquainted with the ancestors of the Teutons would have anticipated for them their glorious contributions to music and metaphysics. Human potentiality is so great, and our knowledge of fundamental racial differences so little, that the cruel repression and extermination of races is not the part of wisdom. A little understanding of human nature and history will enable us to sympathize with the savage and the primitive, the barbarous and the backward, and help us to see that they also in their imperfect fashions are struggling towards that abiding city which shines in dazzling splendour up the steep and narrow way. Every people, every tribe however little advanced in its stage of development, represents a certain psychic type or pattern. The interests of humanity require that every type should be assisted and educated to its adequate expression and development. No race lives to itself and no race dies to itself. Besides, the backwardness of races is due to environmental conditions, physical, social and cultural. Races show considerable powers of adaptation when an external stimulus is applied to them.

When extermination is impossible, the powerful races of the world adopt the second alternative of subordination. They act on the maxim, spare the slave and smash the rebel. The superior races of the world cannot have a clean conscience if they remember their dealings with the coloured ones on the Congo, in Brazil, in Peking at the time of the Boxer revolution, and in America today. For a man like Lord Milner the British Empire meant the *brotherhood* of communities of like *blood* and the mastery of the British race over the non-British dependencies. Civilization is not the suppression of races less capable of or less advanced in culture by people of higher standing. God does not give us the right to destroy or enslave the weak and the unfit. One race may not be as clever or as strong as another, and yet the highest idealism requires that we should give equality of opportunity even to unequal groups. We must respect the independence of every people and lead the backward ones to a full utilization of the opportunities of their environment and a development of their distinctive natural characteristics.

Racial fusion on a large scale is an impossibility, if it is to be achieved in a short period of time. For long centuries of social tradition and natural inheritance have produced marked divergencies of temperament, mentality and physique which cannot be destroyed at a stroke. Nor is it necessary to do away with race individualities and differences to solve the race problem. Uniformity is not the meaning of unity.

In dealing with the problem of the conflict of the different racial groups, Hinduism adopted the only safe course of democracy, viz. that each racial group should be allowed to develop the best in it without impeding the progress of others. Every historical group is unique and specific and has an ultimate value, and the highest morality requires that we should respect its individuality. Caste, on its racial side, is the affirmation of the infinite diversity of human groups. Though the Vedic Aryans started their life in India with a rigid and narrow outlook, regarding themselves as a sort of chosen people, they soon became universal in intention and developed an ethical code applicable to the whole of humanity, a *mānava dharma*. Those who tried to bring together different races in India are worshipped as the makers of the Hindu society. Rāma used the aboriginal tribes in the work of civilizing the South. He brought together the Aryans and the non-Aryans, and so did Kṛṣṇa and the Buddha.

When the aboriginal tribes and others accepted the Hindu standpoint they did not surrender their own individuality but modified it as well as the Hindu spirit which they absorbed. The change is as much in the new group form as in the old ideal. The tribes were admitted into the larger life of Hinduism with the opportunities and the responsibilities which that life gave them, the opportunities to share in the intellectual and cultural life of the Hindus and the responsibilities of contributing to its thoughts, its moral advancement and its spiritual worth—in short, to all that makes a nation's life. Each group dealt with the Hindu ideas in its own characteristic way. We need not overrate the stagnation of the aboriginal tribes. They were also raised above the welter of savagery and imbued with the spirit of gentleness. Sheltered on the same soil, bound together by common interests, evolving under the influence of common psychic and moral surroundings, the different component tribes not only improved in their level but became adapted to each other in spite of diversity of origin. Mr Valentine Chirol remarks: 'The supple and subtle forces of Hinduism had already in prehistoric times welded together the discordant beliefs and customs of a vast variety of races into a comprehensive fabric sufficiently elastic to shelter most of the indigenous populations of India, and sufficiently rigid to secure the Aryan Hindu ascendancy.'[1]

Indiscriminate racial amalgamation was not encouraged by the Hindu thinkers. The Hindu scriptures recognized the rules about food and marriage which the different communities were practising. What we regard as the lower castes have their own taboos and customs, laws and beliefs which they have created for themselves in the course of ages. Every member of the group enters into the possession of the inheritance bequeathed. It is the law of use and wont that distinguishes one group from its neighbours. Caste is really custom. Crude and false as the customs and beliefs of others may seem to us, we cannot deny that they help the community adopting them to live at peace itself and in harmony with others. It is a point of social honour for every member to marry within his own caste, and a 'low' caste woman would refuse to marry one outside her caste, even if he were from a 'higher' one.

Though the Hindu theory of caste does not favour the indiscriminate crossing of men and women, interbreeding has been practised, largely unconsciously, and the essential differences of tribes were modified. Purely anthropological groups are found only among primitive and savage peoples, and not in the societies which play a part in the march of humanity. There has been a general infusion of foreign blood into the Hindu race, and within the race itself there has been a steady flow of blood from the Brahmin to the Caṇḍāla. The inter-mixture of blood has been carefully regulated by means of *anuloma* and *pratiloma* marriages, though the tendency to indiscriminate crossing was not encouraged. While Manu recommends marriages of members of the same caste (*savarṇa*) he tolerates marriages of men with women of the 'lower castes' (*anuloma*). Though he does not justify *pratiloma* marriages, i.e. marriages of women of the 'higher' castes with men of the 'lower', he describes the various progeny of such marriages. While they were not regarded as proper there is no doubt that they prevailed. Castes of a mixed type have been formed in

[1] *India: Old and New* (1921), pp. 42-3.

order to regularize the position of groups originally proceeding from marriages forbidden or discountenanced by custom or law but condoned after a time. Some of the groups which are today regarded as 'untouchable' are said to have arisen by indiscriminate crossing.

While we are dealing with this question, it may be observed that the Hindu system did not condemn all crossing as mischievous. When the stocks are of nearly the same level, crossing is highly beneficial. The deplorable example of the Eurasians is frequently quoted, but then the two stocks happen to be widely different. Besides, the circumstances which accompany their birth and training will damage the best of men. The white man who seduces an Indian nearly always abandons her when she becomes a mother, and the child coming into the world as the product of irregular mating, badly nourished and much despised, grows up generally in conditions which are not very desirable. Not only inheritance but environment also counts.

Yet the principle of *savarṇa* marriages is not unsound. It is a difficult question to decide whether the influence of heredity is so great as to justify *savarṇa* marriages only. The question of nature *versus* nurture is still hotly debated. Democrats are quite certain that it is not blue blood or inherited traits that make for the superiority of the upper classes. The Hindu view, however, has the support of ancient Greek thought and modern science. The Greeks believed in heredity and actually developed a theory of race betterment by the weeding out of inferior strains and the multiplication of the superior ones. As early as the sixth century BC the Greek poet Theognis of Megara wrote, 'We look for rams and asses and stallions of good stock, and one believes that good will come from good; yet a good man minds not to wed the evil daughter of an evil sire. . . . Marvel not that stock of our folk is tarnished, for the good is mingling with the base.' We are all familiar with Plato's views of biological selection as the best method of race improvement. Aristotle also believed that the state should encourage the increase of superior types. There has been during the eighteenth century an increasing insistence on the natural equality of men. Adopting the views of Locke and Rousseau, the thinkers of French and American declarations on human rights, Buckle held that men were moulded by their environments as so much soft clay. Modern science, however, holds that this view exaggerates the influence of the environment. Progress does not depend on a mere change of surroundings. Darwin's teaching that evolution proceeds by heredity was taken up by Galton and other biologists like Weismann and De Vries, and the science of eugenics rests today on somewhat safe and sound foundations. The marvellous potency of the germ-plasm is shown by carefully isolating and protecting it against external influences when it steadily follows its predetermined course. Even when interfered with, it tends to overcome the opposition and resume its normal course. Every cell of our body contains tiny chromosomes, which practically determine our being, height and weight, form and colour, nervous organization and vital energy, temperament and intelligence. Half the number of chromosomes in every cell of our body comes from the father and half from the mother, and they transmit to us most faithfully the qualities of our parents. Any stupidity or insanity of our parents, grandparents or great-grandparents will be transmitted to our children and our children's children. The Hindu thinkers, perhaps through a lucky intuition or an empirical generalization, assumed the fact of heredity and encouraged marriages among those who are of approximately the same type and quality. If a member of a first-class family marries another of poor antecedents the good inheritance of the one is debased by the bad inheritance of the other, with the result that the child starts life with a heavy handicap. If the parents are about the same class the child would be practically the equal of the parents.[1] Blood tells. We cannot make genius

[1] An interesting record of one Martin Kallakak appeared in *Popular Science Siftings*: 'Martin Kallakak was a young soldier in the Revolutionary War. His ancestry was excellent. But in the general laxity and abnormal social conditions of war-time he forgot his noble blood. He met a physically attractive but feeble-minded girl. The result of the meeting was a feeble-minded boy. This boy grew up and married a woman who was apparently

out of mediocrity or good ability out of inborn stupidity by all the aids of the environment.

It does not, however, mean that nature is all and nurture is nothing. The kind of nurture depends on the group and its type. So long as we had the caste system, both nature and nurture co-operated. There is such a thing as social heredity. Each successive generation acquires by conscious effort the social acquisitions of the groups.

If we want to prevent the suicide of the social order, some restrictions have to be observed with regard to marital relations. Marriages should be, not necessarily in one's own caste but among members of approximately the same level of culture and social development. For castes also degenerate. As sons are expected to follow the calling of their fathers, superior individuals are not allowed to grow higher than the groups, and the inferior ones are not allowed to sink lower into their proper scale. Caste, as it is, has not made room for high-born incompetents and low-born talents. While every attempt should be made to energize the weak and the lowly by education and moral suasion, indiscriminate marriage relations do not seem to be always desirable.

Without creating great racial disturbances the Hindu spirit brought about a gradual racial harmony. The synthesis of caste started as a social organization of different ethnic types. There is no doubt that there are many animists who have not been assimilated by Hinduism. When Hindu India lost its independence its work of assimilation and reform stopped,

---

of the same low stock as himself. They produced numerous progeny. These children in turn married others of their kind, and now for six generations this strain has been multiplying. Since that night of dissipation long ago the population has been augmented by 480 souls who trace their ancestry back to Martin Kallakak and the nameless girl. Of these 143 have been feeble-minded, 33 have been immoral, 36 illegitimate, 3 epileptics, 3 criminals and 8 brothel-keepers. The original Martin, however, after sowing this appalling crop of wild oats, finally married a young Quaker woman of splendid talents and noble ancestry. From this union there have been 496 direct descendants. Many of them have been governors, soldiers, one founder of a great university, doctors, lawyers, judges, educators, land-holders, and useful citizens and admirable parents prominent in every phase of social life. The last one in evidence is now a man of wealth and influence.'

though the present day Hindu leaders are slowly realizing their responsibilities towards them.

Caste was the answer of Hinduism to the forces pressing on it from outside. It was the instrument by which Hinduism civilized the different tribes it took in. Any group of people appearing exclusive in any sense is a caste. Whenever a group represents a type a caste arises. If a heresy is born in the bosom of the mother faith and if it spreads and produces a new type, a new caste arises. The Hindu Society has differentiated as many types as can be reasonably differentiated, and is prepared to accept new ones as they arise. It stands for the ordered complexity, the harmonized multiplicity, the many in one which is the clue to the structure of the universe.

Today many brilliant writers are warning us of a world-conflict of races. The rise of racial selfconsciousness is a peculiar phenomenon of our times. The coloured peoples are clamouring rightly for a share in the control of the world. Those who are politically subject are demanding political freedom. The conflict between emigration and immigration countries is highly acute. When the weak, the ignorant and the slothful races were wiped out or subordinated, it was argued in defence of this method that the savage races and the primitive peoples could not expect to remain undisturbed in their habitat, for the world cannot afford to let fields lie fallow and ore remain undug, and if the chance occupants of resourceful areas are too feeble and sluggish to develop them, their displacement by people who can redeem the waste places is necessary and right. The mere fact that in the chance wanderings of the race, a particular tribe happened to pitch its tent on a diamond field or an oil-well whose existence it had not guessed and whose use it had not understood, does not give that tribe an exclusive claim to its possession. No country belongs to itself. The needs of the world are the paramount consideration. But this argument is not applied to the present conditions. While the pressure of population draws masses of men from their countries to seek employment elsewhere, and while there are immense underpopulated areas requiring intelligent labour for the development of their resources, the adjustments are not allowed to take place. America, Australia, South Africa, etc, are forbidden lands to the coloured people. Latin America is very sparsely populated, and might easily contain ten times its present number and increase its production to an almost unlimited extent. There are territories which thirst for population and others which are overflowing with it, and yet pride of race and love of power are overriding all considerations of abstract justice and economic necessity. It is not my purpose here to deal with the practical difficulties in the way of an easy solution of the racial problem. They are great, but they can be solved only by the consciousness of the earth as one great family and an endeavour to express this reality in all our relationships. We must work for a world in which all races can blend and mingle, each retaining its special characteristics and developing whatever is best in it.

Very early in the history of Hinduism, the caste distinctions came to mean the various stratifications into which the Hindu society settled. The confusion between the tribal and the occupational is the cause of the perpetuation of the old exclusiveness of the tribal customs in the still stringent rules which govern the constitution of each caste. Caste on its social side is a product of human organization and not a mystery of divine appointment. It is an attempt to regulate society with a view to actual differences and ideal unity. The first reference to it is in the Puruṣa Sūkta, where the different sections of society are regarded as the limbs of the great self. Human society is an organic whole, the parts of which are naturally dependent in such a way that each part in fulfilling its distinctive function conditions the fulfilment of function by the rest, and is in turn conditioned by the fulfilment of its function by the rest. In this sense the whole is present in each part, while each part is indispensable to the whole. Every society consists of groups working for the fulfilment of the wants of the society. As the different groups work for a common end they are bound by a sense of unity and social brotherhood. The cultural and the spiritual, the military and the political, the economic classes and the unskilled workers constitute the four-fold caste organization. The different functions of the human life were clearly separated and their specific and complementary character was recognized. Each caste has its social purpose and function, its own code and tradition. It is a close corporation equipped with a certain traditional and independent organization, observing certain usages regarding food and marriage. Each group is free to pursue its own aims free from interference by others. The functions of the different castes were regarded as equally important to the well-being of the whole. The serenity of the teacher, the heroism of the warrior, the honesty of the business man, and the patience and energy of the worker all contribute to the social growth. Each has its own perfection.

The rules of caste bring about an adjustment of the different groups in society. The Brahmins were allowed freedom and leisure to develop the spiritual ideals and broadcast them. They were freed from the cares of existence, as gifts to them by others were encouraged and even enjoined. They are said to be above class interests and prejudices, and to possess a wide and impartial vision. They are not in bondage to the State, though they are consulted by the State. The State, as one of the groups in society, was essentially military in its organization. Its specific function was to preserve peace and order, and see to it that the different groups worked in harmony and no confusion of functions arose. The Government was an executive organization expected to carry out the best interests of the people. The Brahmins, as the advisors of the Government, point out the true interests of society.

The political and the economic life of the community is expected to derive its inspiration from the spiritual. This principle saved the State from becoming a mere military despotism. The sovereign power is not identified with the interests of the governing classes but with those of the people at large. While dharma represents the totality of the institutions by which the commonweal is secured and the life of the people is carried on, Government is the political organization which secures for all the conditions under which the best life can be developed. The State did not include the other institutions, trade guilds, family life, etc, which were allowed freedom to manage their own affairs. It did not interfere with art, science and religion, while it secured the external conditions of peace and liberty necessary for them all. Today, the functions of the State are practically unlimited, and embrace almost the whole of social life.

In spite of its attachment to the principle of non-violence, Hindu society made room for a group dedicated to the use of force, the Kṣatriyas. As long as human nature is what it is, as long as society has not reached its highest level, we require the use of force. So long as society has individuals who are hostile to all order and peace, it has to develop controls to check the anti-social elements. These anti-social forces gather together for revolt when the structure of society is shaken by war or internal dissensions. It is a great tribute to the relative soundness of the social structure in Great Britain, in all its strata, that its industrial upheavals, such as the general strike of 1926, which continued for nine days, are marked by little criminality and rowdyism.

The economic group of the Vaiśyas were required to suppress greed and realize the moral responsibilities of wealth. Property is looked upon as an instrument of service. In the great days of Hinduism, the possessor of property regarded it as a social trust and undertook the education, the medical relief, the water supply and the amusements of the community. Unfortunately at the present day in almost all parts of the world the strain of money-making has been so great that many people are breaking down under it. Love of wealth is disrupting social life and is tending to the suppression of the spiritual. Wealth has become a means of self-indulgence, and universal greed is the cause of much of the meanness and cruelty which we find in the world. Hinduism has no sympathy with the view that 'to mix religion and business is to spoil two good things'. We ought not to banish spiritual values from life.

The unskilled workers and the peasants form the proletariat, the Śūdras. These castes are the actual living members of the social body each centred in itself and working alongside one another in co-operation. When a new group is taken into the fold of Hinduism, it is affiliated with one of the four castes. Many of the races from outside were accepted as Kṣatriyas. Mr Jackson writes: 'Those Indians indeed have a poor opinion of their country's greatness who do not realize how it has tamed and civilized the nomads of Central Asia, so that wild Turcoman tribes have been transformed into some of the most famous of the Rajput royal races.'[1]

The system of caste insists that the law of social life should not be cold and cruel competition, but harmony and co-operation. Society is not a field of rivalry among individuals. The castes are not allowed to compete with one another. A man born in a particular group is trained to its manner, and will find it extremely hard to adjust himself to a new way. Each man is said to have his own specific nature (*svabhāva*) fitting him for his own specific function (*svadharma*), and changes of dharma or function are not encouraged. A sudden change of function when the nature is against its proper fulfilment may simply destroy the individuality of the being. We may wish to change or modify our particular mode of being, but we have not the power to effect it. Nature cannot be hurried by our desires. The four castes represent men of thought, men of action, men of feeling, and others in whom none of these is highly developed. Of course, these are the dominant and not the exclusive characters, and there are all sorts of permutations and combinations of them which constitute adulterations (*sankara*) and mixture (*miśra-jāti*). The author of the *Bhagavad-gītā* believes that the divisions of caste are in accordance with each man's character and aptitude.[2] Karma is adapted to *guṇa*, and our qualities in nature can be altered only gradually. Since we cannot determine in each individual case what the aptitudes of the individuals are, heredity and training are used to fix the calling. Though the functions were regarded as hereditary, exceptions were freely allowed. We can learn even

[1] *Indian Antiquary*, January 1911.
[2] iii. 21; xvii. 13, 41, 45-6.

from lowly persons. All people possess all qualities though in different degrees. The Brahmin has in him the possibilities of a warrior. The *ṛṣis* of old were agriculturists and sometimes warriors too.

The caste idea of vocation as service, with its traditions and spiritual aims, never encouraged the notion of work as a degrading servitude to be done grudgingly and purely from the economic motive. The perfecting of its specific function is the spiritual aim which each vocational group set to itself. The worker has the fulfilment of his being through and in his work. According to the *Bhagavadgītā*, one obtains perfection if one does one's duty in the proper spirit of non-attachment. The cant of the preacher who appeals to us for the deep-sea fishermen on the ground that they daily risk their lives, that other people may have fish for their breakfasts, ignores the effect of the work on the worker. They go to sea not for us and our breakfasts but for the satisfaction of their being. Our convenience is an accident of their labours. Happily the world is so arranged that each man's good turns out to be the good of others. The loss of artistic vitality has affected much of our industrial population. A building craftsman of the old days had fewer political rights, less pay and less comfort too, but he was more happy as he enjoyed his work. Our workers who enjoy votes will call him a slave simply because he did not go to the ballot-box. But his work was the expression of his life. The worker, whether a mason or a bricklayer, blacksmith or carpenter, was a member of a great co-operative group initiated into the secrets of his craft at an impressionable age. He was dominated by the impulse to create beauty. Specialization has robbed the worker of pride in craft. Work has now become business, and the worker wants to escape from it and seeks his pleasure outside in cinemas and television. While the social aspirations of the working classes for a fuller life are quite legitimate, there is unfortunately an increasing tendency to interpret welfare in terms of wealth. The claims of materialism are more insistent in the present vision of social betterment. The improvement of human nature is the true goal of all endeavour, though this certainly requires an indispensable minimum of comfort to which the worker is entitled.

We are now face to face with class conflicts. There has grown up an intense class consciousness with elements of suspicion and hatred, envy and jealousy. We are no more content to bring up our children in our own manner of life, but are insisting that all doors must be opened to those equipped with knowledge. The difficulties are due to the fact that some occupations are economically more paying, and all wish to knock at the paying doors. Democracy is so interpreted as to justify not only the very legitimate aspiration to bring about a more equitable distribution of wealth, but also the increasing tendency for a levelling down of all talent. This is not possible. There will always be men of ability who lead and direct, and others who will obey and follow. Brains and character will come to the top, and within the framework of democracy we shall have an aristocracy of direction. It is not true that all men are born equal in every way, and everyone is equally fit to govern the country or till the ground. The functional diversities of workers cannot be suppressed. Every line of development is specific and exclusive. If we wish to pursue one we shall have to turn our attention away from others. While we should remove the oppressive restrictions, dispel the ignorance of the masses, increase their self-respect, and open to them opportunities of higher life, we should not be under the illusion that we can abolish the distinctions of the genius and the fool, the able organizer and the submissive worker. Modern democracies tend to make us all mere 'human beings', but such beings exist nowhere.

India has to face in the near future the perils of industrialism. In factory labour where men are mechanized, where they have little to do with the finished product, and cannot take any pleasure in its production, work is mere labour, and it does not satisfy the soul. If such mechanical work cannot be done by machines, if men have to do it, the less of it they have to do the better for them. The more the work tends to become mechanical and monotonous, the more necessary it is that the worker should have larger leisure and a better equipment for the intelligent use of it. The standard of employment must be raised not merely in wages, but in welfare. Mechanical work should be economically more paying than even that of the artist or the statesman. For in the latter case work is its own reward. In ancient India the highest kind of work, that of preserving the treasures of spiritual knowledge, was the least paid. The Brahmin had no political power or material wealth. I think there is some justice in this arrangement, which shows greater sympathy for those whose work is soul-deadening. We have also to remember that the economic factor is not the most important in a man's life. A man's rank is not to be determined by his economic position. Gambling peers are not higher than honest artisans. The exaltation of the economic will lead to a steady degradation of character. Again, we should not forget that the individuals who constitute the nation cannot all pursue the one occupation of political leadership or military power, but will be distributed into many employments, and these will tend to create distinctive habits and sympathies. Though there may be transfers from one group to another, they are not likely to be numerous.

We are not so certain today as we were a century ago that the individualistic conception of society is the last word in social theory. The moral advantages of the spiritual view of society as an organic whole are receiving greater attention. A living community is not a loose federation of competing groups of traders and teachers, bankers and lawyers, farmers and weavers, each competing against all the rest for higher wages and better conditions. If the members of the different groups are to realize their potentialities, they must share a certain community of feeling, a sense of belonging together for good or evil. There is much to be said from this point of view for the system of caste which adheres to the organic view of society and substitutes for the criterion of economic success and expediency a rule of life which is superior to the individual's interests and desires. Service of one's fellows is a religious obligation. To repudiate it is impiety.

Democracy is not the standardizing of everyone so as to obliterate all peculiarity. We cannot put our souls in uniform. That would be dictatorship. Democracy requires the equal right of all to the development of such capacity for good as nature has endowed them with. If we believe that every type means something final, incarnating a unique possibility, to destroy a type will be to create a void in the scheme of the world. Democracy should promote all values created by the mind. Each kind of service is equally important for the whole. Society is a living organism, one in origin and purpose though manifold in its operations. There can be no real freedom in any section or class in a society so long as others are in bondage. It is a truly democratic ideal that is uttered in the words, 'May all cross safely the difficult places of life, may all see the face of happiness, may all reach that right knowledge, may all rejoice everywhere.' While the system of caste is not a democracy in the pursuit of wealth or happiness, it is a democracy so far as the spiritual values are concerned, for it recognizes that every soul has in it something transcendent and incapable of gradations, and it places all beings on a common level regardless of distinctions of rank and status, and insists that every individual must be afforded the opportunity to manifest the unique in him. Economically we are a co-operative concern or brotherhood where we give according to our capacity and take according to our needs. Politically we enjoy equal rights in the sight of law, and these two enable us to attain true spiritual freedom. A just organization of society will be based on spiritual liberty, political equality and economic fraternity.

In the social order we find that one dominant group invariably subordinates others. Under the feudal constitution of society the exercise of the military function was most esteemed. In modern capitalist organizations wealth dominates. In the Hindu scheme the cultural forms the highest and the economic lowest, for the cultural and the spiritual are ends in themselves and are not pursued for the sake of anything else. The highest in the social hierarchy is the true Brahmin, in whom we find a complete union of opposites, a self-sacrifice which is true freedom, a perfect self-control which is perfect service, absence of personal ambition along with the most intense devotion to the world. The valiant knight, the kṣatriya hero, is not the ideal of India, for he has not the vision of the whole. He identifies himself with one part as against another. He has always something opposed to him which he aims at overpowering. The Brahmin sage who sees the whole of life stands above parties and is centred in the whole surveying all manifestations. He would be untrue to himself if he identified himself with one part as against another. If he does not fight it is not because he rejects all fighting as futile, but because he has finished his fights. He has overcome all dissensions between himself and the world and is now at rest. Both Buddha and Christ were tempted by the Evil One, who had to be defeated before they could obtain freedom. *Maitrī* or friendliness to all is the chief quality of the Brahmin and most of us cannot attain to it except by gradual steps. The good fighter is the preliminary to the wise sage. He who fights gallantly as a warrior gains practical insight through the battlefield and becomes mature for the divine peace of wisdom. Courage on the battlefield manifested in giving and receiving wounds, in dealing death and frankly meeting it, is praised by Aristotle and many militarists. The willingness to sacrifice one's life is the mark of the superior person. Courage becomes the chief virtue of the Kṣatriya, but this type is not the highest, for Kṣatriya valour, however sublimated, is the expression of the primitive in us. We shall have wars and soldiers so long as the brute in us is untamed. Even highly civilized men become brutal at times. The tendency to cruelty is repressed in them rather than outgrown.

In those awful moments of life when the soul stands facing a great wrong and is torn with anguish and indignation the Kṣatriya exclaims: 'Now you shan't do that; I'll kill you', and the true Brahmin will say, 'Do not do that; I would rather die'. The higher the man, the fewer are his rights and the more numerous his duties.

While the dreamer wishes to see his ideals realized immediately and entirely, the Hindu code insists on a gradual transformation. It takes note of the laws and conditions of reality. The misguided idealist is shocked by the imperfections of man, is exasperated by the slow progress achieved, attributes to all his own enthusiasm for ideals, dreams short cuts to the millennium, and thus joins the forces of revolt. The State looks upon him as a danger to society. By protesting against the checks and controls he leaves society open to the assaults of anarchy. The wise plan is to keep our feet on earth and our eyes steady on the stars. Ideals have to be realized through the common clay of human nature, of which the high and the low, the wise and the foolish are made. If all men were wise, life would be a simple task; but as men are attempting to be wise with varying degrees of success, the problems of human life have the character they possess. The Hindu thinkers distinguish between the less evolved in whom the powers of self-analysis and self-direction have not arisen, and the more evolved or the twice-born who were graded into the three classes of Brahmin, Kṣatriya and Vaiśya. The different castes represent members at different stages on the road to self-realization. However lowly a man may be, he can raise himself sooner or later by the normal process of evolution to the highest level and obtain freedom from the vicissitudes of time. Room and time are found for each to take his natural level, and everyone who shows a tendency to rise is lifted to the level of his highest capacity.

Distinctions soon began to be made among the different occupations, and the privileges and restrictions caused the degradation of some groups. Whenever the hierarchical conception tended to endanger the spiritual status and equality of the different classes, protests were uttered. All irrational snobbery was denounced. An artisan is as much a civilized man as a warrior. In the early days of the human race, it is said, there were no class distinctions, since all are born from the Supreme.[1] According to the Śṛuti, the fishermen, the slaves and the gamblers are all divine. The *Bhāgavata* makes out that

[1] sarvam brāhmam idam jagat. *Mahābhārata*. Śanti, p. 186.

there is only one class even as there is only one God. Manu says that all men are born unregenerate (*śūdra*) by the first or physical birth, but become regenerate (*dvija*) by the second or spiritual birth. Caste is a question of character. 'One becomes a Brahmin by his deeds not by his family or birth; even a Caṇḍāla is a Brahmin if he is of pure character.'[1] Some of the great *ṛṣis* worshipped by the Brahmins are half-castes and hybrids. Vaśiṣṭha was born of a prostitute, Vyāsa of a fisher-woman, Parāśara of a Caṇḍāla girl.[2] Conduct counts and not birth. So far as the attainment of perfection is concerned, even the 'low' castes can attain as much as the 'high'. Kṛṣṇa says in the *Bhagavadgītā*, 'Those who take refuge in me even of inferior birth, women and Śūdras, they also attain the highest state.'[3] 'The outcasts who have devotion are entitled to get the saving knowledge through the name of God; women, Śūdras and degraded Brahmins are entitled to get it through the Tantras.'[4] The passion for perfection burns with as keen a flame in the destitute as well as the opulent, the weak as well as the strong. Love is not the possession of a class; nor is imaginative piety a commodity to be bought in markets. Social distinctions disappear so far as these gifts go.

While we all are entitled to perfection, different people are allowed to use the methods which have come down to them through their own group forms. The three upper castes are entitled to obtain perfection through the performance of Vedic sacrifices which the fourth is not allowed to do. *Upanayana* or initiation ceremony and Vedic study were denied to them. Society was perhaps anxious to preserve its useful members from losing their heads over them. Saving knowledge can be gained apart from Vedic study and rights. Śaṁkara allows that Śūdras like Sūta and Vidura obtained the highest knowledge

[1] ix. 14.48.

[2] gaṇikāgarbhasaṁbhūto vaśiṣṭhaś ca mahāmuniḥ
tapasā brāhmaṇo jātaḥ saṁskāras tatra kāraṇaṁ
jātau vyāsastu kaivartyāḥ śvapākyās tu parāśaraḥ.
bahavo'nyepi vipratvam, prāptā ye pūrvam advijāḥ.

[3] ix. 32.

[4] antyajā pi ye bhaktā nāmajñānādhikāriṇah
strīśūdrabrahmabandhūnām tantrajñānādhikāritā.

by virtue of their previous life. Through a study of the Epics and the Purāṇas, through meditation (*japa*), fasting (*upavāsa*), and worship of God (*pūja*) one can attain the Supreme. Every man from the simple fact of his manhood (*puruṣamātra saṁbandhibhiḥ*) is capable of reaching perfection.[1]

The struggle for equality has been with us from the beginning of India's history. We have one evidence of it in the feud between Vaśiṣṭha, the pillar of orthodoxy and the enemy of all innovation, and Viśvāmitra, the leader of the progressives and the champion of freedom and liberty. While the conservative Vaśiṣṭha wanted the Vedic religion to be confined solely to the Aryans, Viśvāmitra tried to universalize it. The movement of the Upaniṣads was in spirit a democratic one. Buddhism, as is well know, undermines all hierarchical ideas. Śaṁkara's philosophy was essentially democratic, and Rāmānuja honoured members of the Śūdra and the Pañcama classes as Ālvārs.

The Vedic rule of life was confined to the people who developed under the stimulus of experience recorded in the Vedas. Its forms are singularly well marked in type, and those of others were sufficiently unlike them to justify a distinction. Each group was allowed to work out its life unfettered by alien ideas which might confuse or obliterate its aim. But soon these special forms were regarded as a sort of spiritual monopoly, and ideas of superiority and inferiority developed. The institution of caste came into being for the development of society,[2] and the welfare of society today demands a breaking down of all suspicion of monopoly. With the general levelling up there will be a greater democratization of the ideals. In the golden age only the Brahmins practised austerities, in the second both Brahmins and Kṣatriyas, in the third the three upper classes, and in the fourth all the four classes. In other words, the Hindu scriptures should be thrown open at the present day to all people irrespective of their caste or sex.

To draw this brief exposition to an end, it may perhaps be

[1] Śaṁkara on *Brahma Sūtra*, iii. 4. 38.
[2] *Manu* i. 32.

useful to give a résumé of the central spirit of Hinduism and its application to the problems of religion and society.

We see that the Hindu recognizes one supreme spirit, though different names are given to it. In his social economy he has many castes, but one society. In the population there are many races and tribes, but all are bound together by one common spirit. Though many forms of marriage are permitted, there is only one ideal aimed at. There is a unity of purpose underlying the multitudinous ramifications.

The world which is a perpetual flow is not all. Its subjection to law and tendency to perfection indicate that it is based on a spiritual reality which is not exhausted in any particular object or group of objects. God is *in* the world, though not *as* the world. His creative activity is not confined to the significant stages in the evolutionary process. He does not merely intervene to create life or consciousness, but is working continuously. There is no dualism of the natural and the supernatural. The spiritual is an emergent of the natural in which it is rooted. The Hindu spirit is that attitude towards life which regards the endless variety of the visible and the temporal world as sustained and supported by the invisible and eternal spirit.

Evil, error and ugliness are not ultimate. Evil has reference to the distance which good has to traverse. Ugliness is half-way to beauty. Error is a stage on the road to truth. They have all to be outgrown. No view is so utterly erroneous, no man is so absolutely evil as to deserve complete castigation. If one human soul fails to reach its divine destiny, to that extent the universe is a failure. As every soul is unlike all others in the world, the destruction of even the most wicked soul will create a void in God's scheme. There is no Hell, for that means there is a place where God is not, and there are sins which exceed his love. If the infinite love of God is not a myth, universal salvation is a certainty. But until it is achieved, we shall have error and imperfection. In a continuously evolving universe evil and error are inevitable, though they are gradually diminishing.

In religion, Hinduism takes its stand on a life of spirit, and affirms that the theological expressions of religious experience are bound to be varied. One metaphor succeeds another in the history of theology until God is felt as the central reality in the life of man and the world. Hinduism repudiates the belief resulting from a dualistic attitude that the plants in my garden are of God, while those in my neighbour's are weeds planted by the Devil which we should destroy at any cost. On the principle that the best is not the enemy of the good, Hinduism accepts all forms of belief and lifts them to a higher level. The cure for error is not the stake or the cudgel, not force or persecution, but the quiet diffusion of light.

In practical religion, Hinduism recognizes that there are those who wish to see God face to face, others who delight in the endeavour to know the truth of it all. Some find peace in action, others in non-action. A comprehensive religion guides each along his path to the common goal, as all woo the same goddess though with different gifts. We must not give supreme and sole importance to our speciality. Perfection can be attained as a celibate, or a householder, or an anchorite. A rigid uniform outlook is wrong. The saintliness of the holy man does not render the steadfastness of the devoted wife or the simple innocence of the child superfluous. The perfection of every type is divine. 'Whatsoever is glorious, good, beautiful and mighty, understand that it goes forth from out of a fragment of my splendour.'[1]

The law of Karma tells us that the individual life is not a term, but a series. Fresh opportunities will be open to us until we reach the end of the journey. The historical forms we assume will depend on our work in the past. Heaven and Hell are higher and lower stages in one continuous movement. They are not external to the experiencing individuals. Purification is by means of purgation. The wages of sin is suffering. We need not regard sin as original and virtue as vicarious. We should do our duty in that state of life to which we happen to be called. Most of us have not a free hand in selecting our vocation. Freedom consists in making the best of what we have, our parentage, our physical nature and mental gifts. Every kind

[1] *Bhagavadgītā*, x. 41.

of capacity, every form of vocation, if rightly used, will lead us to the centre.

While the ideal of monogamy is held up as the best means for a complete mental and spiritual as well as physical understanding between husband and wife, other forms were permitted in view of the conditions of people with different ideals and interests, habits and desires. A happy marriage requires to be made by slow steps and with much patient effort. If incompatibility of temper is enough to justify divorce, many of us will be divorced. While women's functions are distinguished from those of men, there is no suggestion of their inferiority.

While caste has resulted in much evil, there are some sound principles underlying it. Our attitude to those whom we are pleased to call primitive must be one of sympathy. The task of the civilized is to respect and foster the live impulses of backward communities and not destroy them. Society is an organism of different grades, and human activities differ in kind and significance. But each of them is of value so long as it serves the common end. Every type has its own nature which should be followed. No one can be at the same time a perfect saint, a perfect artist, and a perfect philosopher. Every definite type is limited by boundaries which deprive it of other possibilities. The worker should realize his potentialities through his work, and should perform it in a spirit of service to the common weal. Work is craftsmanship and service. Our class conflicts are due to the fact that a warm living sense of unity does not bind together the different groups.

These are some of the central principles of the Hindu faith. If Hinduism lives today, it is due to them, but it lives so little. Listlessness reigns now where life was once like a bubbling spring. We are today drifting, not advancing, waiting for the future to turn up. There is a lack of vitality, a spiritual flagging. Owing to our political vicissitudes, we ignored the law of growth. In the great days of Hindu civilization it was quick with life, crossing the seas, planting colonies, teaching the world as well as learning from it. In sciences and arts, in trade and commerce it was not behind the most advanced nations of the world till the middle of this millennium. Today we seem to be afraid of ourselves, and are therefore clinging to the shell of our religion for self-preservation. The envelope by which we try to protect life checks its expansion. The bark which protects the interior of a tree must be as living as that which it contains. It must not stifle the tree's growth, but must expand in response to the inner compulsion. An institution appropriate and wholesome for one stage of human development becomes inadequate and even dangerous when another stage has been reached. The cry of conservatism 'it has always been thus' ignores the fundamentals of the theory of relativity in philosophy and practice, in taste and morals, in politics and society, of which the ancient Hindus had a clear grasp. The notion that in India time has stood still for uncounted centuries, and nought has been changed since the primeval sea dried up, is altogether wrong. While there has been continuity with the past, there has also been progress. The Upaniṣads are products of a perfectly spiritual movement which implicitly superseded the cruder ceremonial religion of the Vedas. When the movement of the Upaniṣads became lost in dogmatic controversies, when the fever of disputes and dialectics lulled the free spirit of religion, Buddhism called upon the people to adhere to the simplicity of truth and the majesty of the moral law. About the same period, when canonical culture and useless learning made religion inhuman scholasticism, and filled those learned in this difficult trifling with ridiculous pride, the *Bhagavadgītā* opened the gates of heaven to all those who are pure in heart. When the ritualists succeeded in imprisoning the living faith in rigid creeds, the true prophets of the spirit, the Śaiva and the Vaiṣṇava saints, and the theologians like Śaṁkara and Rāmānuja, summoned the people to the worship of the living God. The influence of Madhva and Caitanya, Basava and Rāmānanda, Kabīr and Nānak is not inconsiderable. There has been no such thing as a uniform stationary unalterable Hinduism whether in point of belief or practice. Hinduism is a movement, not a position; a process, not a result; a growing tradition, not a fixed revelation. Its past history encourages us to believe that it will be found equal to any emergency that the future may throw up, whether in the field of thought or of history.

After a long winter of some centuries, we are today in one of the creative periods of Hinduism. We are beginning to look upon our ancient faith with fresh eyes. We feel that our society is in a condition of unstable equilibrium. There is much wood that is dead and diseased that has to be cleared away. Leaders of Hindu thought and practice are convinced that the times require, not a surrender of the basic principles of Hinduism, but a restatement of them with special reference to the needs of a more complex and mobile social order. Such an attempt will only be the repetition of a process which has occurred a number of times in the history of Hinduism. The work of readjustment is in process. Growth is slow when roots are deep. But those who light a little candle in the darkness will help to make the whole sky aflame.

*Also published as Mandala Books*

**AN IDEALIST VIEW OF LIFE**

Radhakrishnan

'The most complex statement of religion in the language of the present day that I have read.'

*Everyman*

'Science is a system of second causes, which cannot describe the world adequately, much less account for it.' Radhakrishnan explores in *An Idealist View of Life* modern intellectual debate and the vain attempts to find a substitute for religion. He discusses, drawing upon the traditions of East and West, the nature and validity of religious experience. Finally, he creates a fine vision of man's evolution and the emergence of higher values. The range of subject combined with the author's own living faith, undogmatic and free of creed, makes this book a philosophical education in itself.

**ESSENTIALS OF INDIAN PHILOSOPHY**

M. Hiriyanna

This book provides both the general reader and student with a concise and easily understood account of Indian philosophy. It begins with early Indian thought, summarises Vedic religion and philosophy and goes on to deal with the great scholastic systems of Indian thought which evolved after the close of the Vedic period. Historical surveys accompany each main division of the subject. The number of Sanskrit terms that appear in the text have been reduced as far as possible but a glossary of them together with the subject-index are included.

**RAMAṆA MAHARSHI**
The Sage of Aruṇācala

T. M. P. Mahadevan

Ramaṇa Maharshi, the sage of Aruṇācala, has long been regarded as the most saintly of modern Hindu ascetics and mystics. He is also one of the most intriguing.

At the age of seventeen, in 1896, he was suddenly seized by an overwhelming desire to visit Tiruvaṇṇāmalai or Aruṇācala, a sacred hill many miles from his home. There he began his life of contemplation and for seventeen years lived in a cave.

Many people visited the sage, ranging from peasants and *sādhus* to writers and statesmen. Among them were Somerset Maugham, Arthur Osborne and Paul Brunton, who helped bring his teaching to the Western world.

The philosophy of Ramaṇa Maharshi is outstanding for its purity and gentleness. Like St Francis of Assisi he loved animals and is said to have exercised an almost supernatural hold over them. He preached that God, the self and the world are indivisible and advocated a life of tranquillity, non-violence and meditation.

**SAMADHI**

The Superconsciousness of the Future

Mouni Sadhu

Samadhi means 'superconsciousness'. Writing directly from his own experience, Mouni Sadhu, the well-known author of *The Tarot*, *Concentration*, *Meditation* and *In Days of Great Peace*, demonstrates the way to develop a keener sense of awareness, the means of transcending the dichotomy between body and mind and the method of achieving a lasting sense of spirituality and inner peace. Based on the methods of the author's own spiritual mentor, Ramaṇa Maharshi, *Samadhi* is a practical manual leading to clear and scientific conceptions about the different forms of consciousness.

'The author's exposition of the subject is masterly. Here we have a subject which, by its very nature, is difficult to explain in words, dealt with with unparalleled clarity and simpleness which it is within the means of anyone to understand.'

*Middle Way*